I0485089

SOUL SURVIVAL IN
CORPORATE AMERICA

SOUL SURVIVAL IN CORPORATE AMERICA

A Woman's Story of Business Success and
Inner Peace

Lynne Leahy

SOUL SURVIVAL IN CORPORATE AMERICA
A WOMAN'S STORY OF BUSINESS SUCCESS AND INNER PEACE

Copyright © 2004, 2014 Lynne Leahy.

All rights reserved. No part of this book may be used or reproduced by any means, graphic, electronic, or mechanical, including photocopying, recording, taping or by any information storage retrieval system without the written permission of the publisher except in the case of brief quotations embodied in critical articles and reviews.

iUniverse books may be ordered through booksellers or by contacting:

iUniverse LLC
1663 Liberty Drive
Bloomington, IN 47403
www.iuniverse.com
1-800-Authors (1-800-288-4677)

Because of the dynamic nature of the Internet, any web addresses or links contained in this book may have changed since publication and may no longer be valid. The views expressed in this work are solely those of the author and do not necessarily reflect the views of the publisher, and the publisher hereby disclaims any responsibility for them.

Any people depicted in stock imagery provided by Thinkstock are models, and such images are being used for illustrative purposes only. Certain stock imagery © Thinkstock.

ISBN: 978-0-5953-1555-0 (sc)
ISBN: 978-0-5957-7805-8 (hc)
ISBN: 978-0-5957-6369-6 (e)

Printed in the United States of America.

iUniverse rev. date: 08/04/2014

Contents

The Corporate Abyss

Soon after I landed my first big corporate job, I began to have some business success. It didn't come easily. With little formal education, I felt I needed to work extra hours to get onto an even playing field with my peers. I did like the challenge of corporate life. I also loved the men, the parties, the cocktail hour, and the two-martini lunches. I had stepped to the edge of the abyss and I didn't even know it yet. Business success was like an exotic hallucinogenic drug, but it was never enough for me. It never lasted long enough. My soul was deteriorating under the relentless pursuit of improved financial performance.

A dark, secret feeling of inadequacy haunted me. As I tumbled over the edge, I struggled to fight the downward spiral into an emotional abyss.

As long as I could get up in the morning, put on that conservative business suit, and get to the office with briefcase in hand, I was able to keep up a respectable and competent facade. I kept everyone believing that I was all right. Even as the powerful spiral of the abyss sucked me more swiftly down toward ultimate emotional destruction, I was able, day after day, to put on the corporate costume. I reassured everyone that I was doing just fine. After all, I was one of the young shining stars in the company.

Out of the office, my life was a shameful and devastating mess. After each episode of desperate emotional struggle, I would "get myself together," put on the corporate costume, put my business cards in my wallet (so I could remember who I was), and return to my desk.

I continued to show up with the corporate smile and continued to do the work better than many in my office. My co-workers continued to close their eyes to my dreadful emotional condition.

My soul, the core of my being, was fighting for survival.

If you are free-falling into an abyss, let go. Move into *Soul Survival* mode. Struggling is useless. Let go of all of the old ideas that are strangling you. If you are facing a corporate layoff or if you are miserably unhappy and unfulfilled in your corporate position, this can be your greatest moment. Corporate life is what we make it, but often our attitudes are full of fear and fear blocks the light of reason and hope.

Everyone I know who has been downsized out or bludgeoned to insanity by corporate life and has had the courage to remain vigilant and open has, without exception, been brought to a new and more meaningful place in his or her career.

Practicing the *Soul Survival* spiritual principles will help you manifest the changes you wish to see in the corporate world, and then your daily work life will take on rich and enduring purpose.

Soul Survival in Corporate America will shock you, entertain you, encourage you, and inspire you so that you never again have to hide anything about yourself anywhere; at work, at home, with friends, and with strangers.

Excerpts from Soul Survival in Corporate America

Acknowledgements

I want to thank my women friends (*soul survivors*, one and all), my family, my friends, and my business associates, who've continued to believe in my book and have encouraged me to not ever give up. I am blessed with so many supporters that I can't name them all here but they have been the "wind beneath my wings." They have loved me unconditionally. They have seen the best in me when times were good and when times were tough. I am grateful to you all.

I especially want to thank Mary Ann Gutoff, Lori Wong, Barbara Yanowski, Randy Brown, Linda Ipsen, Kiki Humrich, and Kiki Dowd for their outstanding creative and technical skills that helped me finally put all of my thoughts and experiences into this book and get it ready for publication. Their talent and unwavering attention to detail has been invaluable to me.

I also want to acknowledge all of the businesswomen trudging the corporate road who have continued to aspire toward their dreams. You are my inspiration. If my experiences, now put to paper, can help even one woman somewhere feel less alone, less afraid, and more courageous about their future, and their ability to succeed peacefully and powerfully, then I am truly grateful. This book is dedicated to you.

A percentage the profits from Soul Survival in Corporate America will be divided between Hope House and WISE (Women's Initiative for Self Employment).

Hope House, in Redwood City, CA is a recovery home and refuge for women who've fallen over the edge of the abyss and lost all hope. In this amazing house, women find honesty, self-esteem, and the courage to dream new dreams. It has been my gift to be a part of Hope House and to see the ongoing miracle of recovery.

WISE (San Francisco) is one of the foremost programs in the United States for inspiring and teaching low-income women how to build successful, self-supporting businesses. WISE is dedicated to helping low-income, under-privileged women rise above their seemingly hopeless conditions and aspire to business and financial success.

Introduction

I was eleven years old that bright sunny day in May, innocently walking home from the school bus stop. My old yellow dog, Posey, always met me about half way home, with tail wagging and a mouth full of slobbery kisses. This day, Posey did not come to meet me. A car had hit Posey. Posey was dead.

Three weeks later, I arrived home alone, and my daddy was not there. They had taken my daddy to jail. Daddy was gone.

Suffering from an already worn-out, worried little heart housed in my small, fragile child's body, I decided not to feel anymore. I decided not to feel fear, loss, pain, or any other feeling that scared me. I decided then, at the age of eleven, that if I were going to survive in this world, I'd have to toughen up, to get brave, to have courage. I thought it was a noble decision.

That was the beginning of an eighteen-year, futile odyssey that took me through the gates of Hell. It was also the necessary down payment on a life that is more wonderful than my wildest dreams; a life of success and joy, a life filled with feeling.

This book is about two journeys. The first, a twenty-nine year trek through the loneliness and pain of a completely failed and fear ridden life; the second, a twenty-nine year pathway of joy, success, and fulfillment. In my mind, it is nearly impossible to separate one from the other. They were intricately woven into the whole.

- At 17, I was a high school dropout and never expected to amount to anything—at 35, I was a corporate superstar, professionally acclaimed throughout a multinational Fortune 500 company.

- At 25, I was a single mom with 2 children, living on welfare, filled with fear and insecurity—today, I have founded and operated five successful businesses and live in financial security.

- At 28, while incarcerated and wrapped in a straightjacket, I was diagnosed with irreparable mental and emotional disorders—now I am an example of spiritual healing and incredible peace and happiness.

- At 29, I was hopelessly addicted to drugs and alcohol—today, I have lived clean and sober for over 30 years.

And now I am at the beginning again. At 59 years of age, I am beginning the third-third of my life and here's the irony; I am more enthusiastic about life than ever before. I'm excited about my career, my family, and my new goals.

I've written this book to all of the beings out there who are struggling with their careers, their finances, their dreams, their ambitions, their beliefs, and their fears. In this book, I share with you my journey to peace and a personally defined success. I hope this book inspires you to live in the story that is your life and to find out the inevitable truth that nothing happens in God's world by mistake. Your *divine destiny* is not a place to get to, but a path to travel.

1

Soul Survival in Corporate America

I am the consummate corporate citizen. I first got into the business world because I had to survive as a single mom and feed my family. Ultimately, I became a passionate and successful leader, entrepreneur, and businessperson. This is the story of how I rose out of the depths of fear, insecurity, and depression to learn to enjoy, embrace, and honor each moment of the life I've been given.

Every day people put on a corporate costume, go to their jobs, and give away precious hours, days, and years of their lives to careers, corporations, and principles they do not believe in or really care about. They are being strangled by the corporate culture. Corporate life today is strewn with tragedies like these:

- A Fortune 500 Corporate Division President is found dead by his teenage son, a shotgun nearby where it lurched from his mouth after he had pulled the trigger committing suicide.

- A seemingly extraordinary department manager mentally isolates to the extreme and walks out the door never to return to corporate life.

- A highly capable young woman never rises to her obvious exceptional business abilities. Everyone wonders why.

- The most talented salesperson in the department cannot sustain quota performance without a jigger of gin before work.

1

- The brilliant engineer, seeking stock options and early retirement, is now in a corporate slot doing boring, repetitive production line work as his health deteriorates from stress.

In my third year as a corporate citizen, I put over a hundred sleeping pills in my mouth and swallowed them. Unlike the Fortune 500 Executive mentioned above, I survived to learn these lessons and tell this tale.

Stress, depression, suicide, sexual abuse, alcoholism, addiction, personal tragedies are all unspeakable issues in corporate life. Talking openly about these things can save our own sanity and the lives and spirits of many of the people we touch each day. If we can open up this honest dialog, corporations will thrive as never before. They will thrive through the spiritual energy and love that empowers individuals to seek their highest potential.

Getting Real at Work

Is it safe to be real at work? To be kind, honest, generous, whole, and authentic? Most workers in corporate life believe it is not safe. There is a perverse, controlling undercurrent of stressful phoniness that drives corporate culture. It is the bogyman of business that scares people at work. It is a bogyman because it is not real.

I have experimented for thirty years, living a full-on, honest, feet-in-the-street corporate life, and it has been a miraculous spiritual adventure. I have had an enviable career filled with success, achievement, and respect. The underground, unsafe phony atmosphere created by the competitiveness, fear, and ego of corporate culture is nothing but a bogyman.

If you seek a meaningful spiritual life, how can you live a fake life at work? For most of us our work life is the larger part of our existence. Why should it be anything less than authentic, spiritual, and fulfilling? Living in the *Soul Survival* principles will encourage you to insist upon a full life for yourself—with honesty, love, and fulfillment as the foundation for every minute of your existence on this earth.

Dec. 6, 1973—It would be hard for anyone to believe the events of that day—the day my rocket ride began as a business superstar and one of the first women in Corporate America to reach the uncharted territory of corporate stardom with a Fortune 500 company. How could what I was about to do result in extraordinary business success? This was definitely not one of Dale Carnegies' tips on *How to Win Friends and Influence People*[1].

I was so sick, I could hardly stand up. I had spent thirty minutes in the shower trying to wash away the smell of stale vodka and wine seeping out of my pores. My knees were weak and my stomach was lurching like I had swallowed an out-of-control boomerang. With bloodshot eyes, I looked pitiful, bedraggled, and old. I was twenty-nine. It seemed that my short corporate career was coming to a sad end.

I walked into the prestigious mahogany-row office of the Corporate Vice President. My voice quivered pathetically as I said, "I think I have a problem with alcohol. I might be an alcoholic and possibly a drug addict as well." This admission was not an act of courage. I just could not go on any longer living a lie. At the bottom depths of despair, depression, and desperation, no one could hurt me anymore than I had hurt myself. In my four corporate years I had attempted suicide eight times, had been locked up countless times in psychiatric wards, worn straight jackets, been administered drug treatments and shock treatments, and had humiliated myself, my boss, and my company. Helpless and hopeless, I could not scheme one more scheme, cook up one more deal, or make up one more story.

Only four years earlier, I had been a high school drop out, living on welfare, trying to keep two preschool children and myself afloat. This big corporate job had been a very fortunate break for me. But alas, I clearly could not handle it.

I assumed I would be fired that day. It was what I expected and deserved. I had missed days, no, actually weeks of work. I was unaccountable and unreliable. I was a disgrace to myself and ashamed beyond belief. All the fight was gone out of me. I could only tell the truth and live with the consequences. At that point, the most unexpected thing happened.

My boss said, "Lynne, I had been prepared to fire you today—BUT if you are ready to be honest and try to do something about your problem, I will stick by you for awhile."

The miracle of this story was not just a miracle for me; it was also a miracle for my boss and that corporation. It was at the same corporation just three years later that I became one of the highest producers of new business in the history of the company. By 1979 I was recognized as the National leader in corporate sales. No woman had ever achieved this performance level before. In 1981 I became the first woman member of the prestigious President's Club, an

---

1.   Dale Carnegie, *How to Win Friends and Influence People*, Simon & Schuster, 1936

honor defined by five continuous years of being in the top 25% of corporate performers.

It all happened because finally, I had been honest in confronting myself and the company with the real-deal. Becoming honest and spiritually authentic had been good for me and good for the company. A profound shift had taken place deep within my soul. Going forward from that day I knew if I were to survive, I would need that same degree of honesty every moment of every day. I felt like a turtle walking into the corporate world without a shell.

Soul Survival reports the outcome of that incredible thirty-year experiment and shares a set of principles and a confidence building system that will bring anyone success. More importantly, living by these principles will align you with your true purpose in life, your divine destiny. When you live in harmony with your true-life purpose you will know joy beyond comprehension.

The simple principles outlined in the book will enable you to create just-in-time miracles so you will never again have to worry about saying the wrong thing or making a bad decision.

Your Authenticity Can Change Corporations Forever

Soul Survival starts with being rigorously honest with yourself. Unless you can learn to be honest with yourself, you won't truly know yourself. Without self-knowledge, your actions, thoughts, and decisions are centered on external circumstances instead of your internal spiritual consciousness. Being honest means seeing yourself in the world as clearly as possible. Once you examine and dispel the illusions that you hold about yourself, you free yourself to live a more genuine life. Being honest about everything opens the door to the soul. Honesty is about rediscovering your authentic self, thereby clearing your vision about what is true for you, and in business; what constitutes right action for you.

Honesty in dealing with others flows naturally from self-honesty. When you are clear about what is true for you, and you have a clear connection with your personal truth, you have easy internal access to what is right or wrong for you, making it simpler to act with integrity. Acting from your authentic self, you will know your personal bottom line and you will be aware of actions that are unacceptable to you.

If you, as a single individual, can be brave enough to be genuine in your business dealings, you can change the way corporations do business forever. No, I'm not joking. Your honesty, your compassion and your willingness to be vulnerable in the presence of your colleagues is tremendously powerful medicine for the corporate world. It has the power to lift us all out of typical corporate lives of phoniness, pretense, materialism, and egotism to those of genuine satisfaction and meaningful work. And it is so much easier to explore your warts when you see others do so and thrive.

In 1973 I had a profound experience, a miracle if you like, and it happened right in the middle of mainstream Corporate America. Since that time, I've been living in Corporate America like a turtle without a shell. My personal life and my professional life have blurred together into a single spiritual adventure.

Since then the people whom I have worked for and the people who have worked for me have known exactly who I am and how I feel. They've known about my devastation over business failures, my battles with alcoholism and drug addiction, my despair about divorce, my struggles as a single parent, my healing from sexual abuse, my failures, my illnesses, my lack of education, my insecurities, my victories, my fears, my beliefs, my dreams for my future, and on and on. And my clients have known at some level that I am striving to bring them not just products and services, but the best I can offer as a human being in a spirit of love and kindness.

I know some readers will balk at these ideas:

- If I am honest, if I am real at work, then I'll be scorned or fired or considered a weakling. Then what will I do?

- I'll become vulnerable to politics and lose my position.

- They'll stab me in the back.

Each may be true. Are you willing to move in the direction of a more authentic life, all day, every day? If so, you may be willing to opt for the freedom that spiritual authenticity offers. As a result, you may, in fact, change jobs, change careers, and even become who you want to be. Is this a chance you are willing to take? After all, isn't that better than living a half-life, hiding in the phoniness of some day-to-day corporate cultures? If you can't be who you are at work, then how can you thrive and grow in that environment?

Look at it this way. We are all created with a magnificent, talented, loving spirit inside. We are created with everything we need for a happy and fulfilling life. Sometimes it takes a big leap of faith to make room for that spirit to come forth and shine. I needed to be flat on my back before I was able to look up and see the sun shining. I had to be ready to accept being fired or scorned. *Soul*

Survival offers you the story of one corporate traveler who learned that princi-ples are more important than any glistening corporate prize.

The remainder of this book recounts my experiences and the experiences of others who have had the courage to share them. We discovered these powerful principles as we climbed the corporate ladder, raised families, rallied through suicidal depressions, addictions, relentless fear and shame, and sought to build lives of success. These personal anecdotes are meant to illustrate that all of life is a spiritual process and that no experience is wasted when we seek the lessons in it. Regardless of how we come into this world, we can make the most of ourselves and connect with others in loving and productive ways.

The Power of Personal Stories

This book is mostly my story. It is not a story about a mighty mogul of corpo-rate success but it is instead, about an ordinary person like yourself having extraordinary experiences within the day-to-day life of an average corporate citizen and businessperson. I pray this story will bring hope to anyone strug-gling to define his or her own life and inner spirit-self while traveling through this fast-paced, technological corporate maze.

It was not intended that this would be a "women's story," but of necessity, (I am a woman), the story contains some experiences that are unique to women. That said, my observation is that when the soul-level lessons are reached, gender issues are neutralized. Male and female souls alike search for deep inner peace, love, and acceptance. My male friends who have had the courage to touch their inner true selves admit to the same fears and struggles that I have tangled with during my journey.

Although there were times when I seriously questioned my sanity at remaining in this sometimes seemingly godless, day to day corporate life, I have remained in the middle of corporate life with the determined idea that even those of us existing and driving through this strange corporate milieu are human beings with souls and spiritual longings that don't materialize on the corporate balance sheet, the year-end incentive bonus or the good old depend-able paycheck.

By sticking with my high-risk, spiritual adventure through the corporate world, I have had an extraordinary career. I fully expect this journey to bring even greater joys and adventures. The corporate world is my marathon course—my survival trek. The adventures and challenges of this course will enrich my spirit and stretch my soul beyond my wildest dreams. As I seek to grab the gold ring of success, I will discover that my spiritual contribution to the people who cross my path is more important than any material prize.

Scientists, doctors, and MBA's cite cases, discuss theory, and offer us intellectual direction for living our lives. But each of us has our own simple, meaningful story. Our shared stories of business and personal successes and failures break the sense of isolation that prevents us from knowing how similar so many of our challenges are. When we know we are not alone and our experiences are not unique, we are buoyed by the knowledge that others have gone before us and survived. Our stories are the greatest gifts we can give to one another.

Sharing the tough stuff of how I became who I am today will remind you that nothing is wasted when we learn from it. Many of my life lessons were learned with my feet on the street in the daily fray of corporate strife and competition. I have learned that in every encounter, I have the power to choose my behavior, my purpose, and ultimately the kind of person I become. Will I go forward, striving for gluttonous material gain and profit? Or will I go forward, open and vulnerable, to experience the love and spiritual adventure with the human beings I meet along the way?

The trials and tribulations of climbing out of the depths of hopelessness have educated my soul with rich and rewarding lessons. The two most valuable experiences in my life to date have been the toughest ones. I call them my *abyss experiences*. Yes, I'm grateful to have raised good children and I'm glad to have shared part of my life with a soul mate. I'm happy to have a rewarding career, and yet I wouldn't trade my abyss experiences, my earth-shattering crises, for anything, because it was during those times that I was introduced to my soul, my life purpose, the depth of my character, and my loving creator.

The scary issues we all face (the IRS, company layoffs, job performance reviews, business failures, corporate political battles, economic issues, bankruptcy, death, sickness, addiction, divorce; the endless list of troubles that all of us go through) are not unique. Many have gone before us and have survived. We, too, will go on and find hope, new values, and deeper meaning to our lives. I hope that my stories show that we are each far stronger than our human systems would have us believe. We are unexplored bottomless vessels of spiritual power.

As the saying goes, we are not mere human beings having *spiritual* adventures. We are magnificent and bold spiritual beings having exciting *human* adventures. If we allow it, our business lives can provide fertile grounds for great and challenging spiritual journeys. In the pages that follow, I will share some stories and the lessons I learned from my journey with you.

2

Is Your Corporate Life a Mistake or Your Mission?

Peace of mind and financial success are not mutually exclusive. You can have both. This book gives you a tried-and-true system that is simple to practice every day. The *Soul Survival* principles are not easy but they are simple. If practiced, you will find harmony with your soul and flourish in your career.

I am the President/CEO of a multi-million dollar health technology company. For a long time I thought my life was a mistake. When I began my corporate climb I was a twenty-five year-old single parent of two pre-school children living on welfare, food stamps, and the kindness of strangers. How I made that corporate climb with a full and joyous heart is the lesson of this book. If I can do it, anyone can—most certainly you, if that is your desire.

In this just-in-time society, it is easy to be seduced by the glitter of material and financial success. These rewards are shallow. The only true success is a singing heart. Financial success can't assure a happy life but internal confidence can. Money can't buy a full and joyous life but the simple principles in this book, if practiced, will assure you of all of these rewards.

With super-sonic speed, fortunes are made or lost by the movement of a decimal point in the stock market. Just-in-time manufacturing, just-in-time shipping, just-in-time printing, and just-in-time almost everything makes the business world move so fast our heads spin.

Today, I fly in corporate jets, drive my cherished BMW, and vacation in paradise. However, I need to know that with or without these material pleasures my heart will still be joyous and full. *Soul Survival*, just-in-time miracles,

9

and practicing the simple principles outlined in this book promise that. So read this book, practice these principles, and, as I have done, you will find your life is not a mistake but a mission.

The spiritual principles outlined in this book are the basis of a simple belief system that will enable you to make bold and inspired decisions. Many people like myself, did not grow up in an environment that equipped us with the internal confidence to know absolutely, that our decisions and strategies were indeed worthy of business and financial success. Even individuals with solid business educations often find themselves unsure in a just-in-time world where if you falter or hesitate, you are sure to be left behind.

My passion to live a spiritually integrated life has been my blessing—or my burden—depending upon the moment. My mentors often have admonished me for being too much the crusader, yet I value my passionate nature because my intensity has guided me to my lessons and challenges for spiritual growth. My passion has shown the way to peaceful union of all of the sacred moments of my life. My passion has driven me to seek it all, to believe I could have a spiritually centered life in which my corporate vocation is as much my destiny as my motherhood and my marriage. I believe that the integration of these significant life compartments is nothing less than a sacred mission.

I was the woman dubbed "Least Likely to Succeed," and I surely had a knapsack of excuses blocking my pathway to fulfillment. Growing up in a broken home and an alcoholic family, I was the eldest of three. My father went to prison when I was eleven, I dropped out of high school at sixteen, married at seventeen, and found myself alone, uneducated, penniless, and on welfare with two babies at the age of twenty-five. The only self-image I had was that I was a loser. In my mind, I was clearly doomed. To succeed was to survive in those days. Survival was my primary goal. Success beyond survival felt so distant that I couldn't begin to consider it and awareness of my own spirituality had never even occurred to me.

Today, I am a mother, a corporate super-achiever, a several-times successful entrepreneur, an author, a seminar speaker, a marathon runner, a yoga student, and a happy human being. I am writing a fourth book and actively leading a rapidly growing business. My spiritual consciousness is intimately interwoven into each of these life roles.

I am also a grandmother, a trusted and reliable friend, a family member, a contributing member of society, and an active member of a spiritual community. I adore my children and grandchildren. My spiritual community feeds my soul on a regular basis.

Each of these roles can be a full-time, demanding challenge, but my experience has taught me about the bigger picture of integrating them into a prosperous, successful, and fulfilling life. That is what this book is about. I want no walls between the parts of my life. I want to feel as passionately about negotiating business deals in an honorable and honest way as I feel about holding my grandchild and sharing a celebration or a tragedy with one of my children. I want the flow from each part of my life to be unencumbered as I move through the day. I want to have a life that counts, every minute of it. I want a life of meaning. I have found such a life over the course of my journey as a businessperson within the corporate structure and as a citizen living in a corporate society. The challenges I've encountered and the soul lessons I've learned in business helped me to evolve and eventually to flourish in my life.

Many people today compartmentalize their lives into what they consider manageable segments: home, church, family, job, etc. A successful businessperson may be unhappy in the home compartment, a successful mother may find emptiness in the career compartment, a successful corporate achiever may lack a meaningful relationship with another person, and a gentle artistic soul may crumble under the weight of economic survival. Erecting these rigid compartments leaves people feeling isolated and confused.

This is not a book about finding balance in your life. I believe trying to attain balance between work, family, friends, relaxation, and spirituality is a futile exercise in effort and control. Trying to achieve balance is like the concept of dieting. Diets don't work because disciplines of control and effort are rigid, impossible to maintain, and confining to the growth of your soul. The soul is a fluid and expansive guide when you learn to trust the process of responding to your heart and following its lead.

The concept of balance supposes that as human beings, we have remarkable powers to segregate our lives into compartments and then adjust our personalities to fit the compartment we're in at a given moment. Both career success and personal peace have come into my life not through control and discipline, but through surrender, humility, and open-mindedness; a gentler approach to intense living and rigid compartmentalized roles.

This book is a flexible formula for living a life in which every minute of each day is precious and meaningful to your innermost being, your *soul self.* Every part of your life is precious, whether it is witnessing your five-year-old child's newfound ability to spell or negotiating a loan for your business with your banker or slogging through a bone-crushing personal depression or being challenged at the office by an insecure co-worker.

The *Soul Survival* principles offer tools to help you unite all aspects of your life into a full and meaningful adventure. The stories share simple spiritual ideas that can transform your life in ways that feel miraculous. These five principles will bring about amazing events and clear a peaceful path through the insanity of cutthroat, competitive 21st Century corporate life.

All of life is a spiritual experience. When we try to separate our work-related interactions from our spiritual experiences, we rob ourselves of the opportunity to see our co-workers as spiritual partners in our lives.

When we view business experiences as spiritual experiences, no less precious to our hearts and essential to our spiritual growth than our experiences with loved ones, we can begin to treat ourselves, our co-workers, and the workplace with the compassion, respect, and depth each deserves.

When we stop separating our spiritual selves from the rest of our lives, we begin to see that our workplace is simply another environment for learning to love and honor our journey. Co-workers and business associates are fellow travelers on our spiritual path. They have something to teach us and we have something to teach them—and not just about the bottom line. Our lessons are about love, power, control, compassion, anger, and courage. Co-workers take on new significance when we view them in the light of spiritual teachers. Knowing that all of life is a spiritual journey elevates the workplace into yet another *classroom for the soul.*

Working from the heart (the communication to soul) makes me a better businesswoman. I get better financial results, I make clear and powerful decisions, and I establish lasting relationships with clients and fellow workers. And my family has respect for my career life, not just as a means to put a roof over our heads, but as an important part of my spiritual development.

When I work from my heart, my core strengths shine through and success is a natural outcome. While corporate polish may snag an apple or two, working from the heart lands the entire tree. Great success and immense satisfaction come from being completely honest and loving with business associates. Clients and business associates whose relationships have been forged in love and trust are also the most enduring relationships of all.

The Value of Business Relationships Forged in Trust

In 1981, I was at the peak in my career with a particular Fortune 500 company. I had succeeded in a niche of the technology industry where no woman had succeeded before. I had surpassed everyone in the company in sales and new business. I was respected and had established many strong business relationships with executives from major banks and corporations.

Being a woman and a visible achiever was not easy. Some co-workers were jealous and vindictive. I worked in a company where the *Peter Principle*[1] was practiced.[2] Insecure and incompetent people were often promoted into management. My success felt threatening to some of these managers, and as a result, I was being pressured by people who had essentially failed at the job I was doing so well.

Year-end 1981—Management came to me offering to make some concessions on payment schedules if I could persuade one of my major accounts (an international bank) to accept shipment on a large order that would be designated for branch use in the upcoming year. I knew I would be getting the business, either now or next year. I didn't have a big stake in getting the early order. My management was using a common corporate tactic to inflate year-end numbers and thereby increase their bonuses. I always tried to be a team player, so I went along with the program.

I went to the client, an Executive Vice President of the bank, and proposed the plan. He respected and trusted me. We had been doing business for several years and I had never let him down. I also liked and respected him. We had a solid business relationship. He agreed to the plan. I entered his order with the understanding that the bank wouldn't have to pay for the equipment until later in the year when they actually put it to use in their branch operations.

As it turned out, my management never cleared their little *pump up the year-end numbers* scheme with the accounting department. When the invoices came due in 30 days, I got a call from the accounting department asking me why my client hadn't paid the bill. I explained about my management's agreement for the client to pay later. This caused a horn-locking, ego battle between the executives in sales and the executives in accounting. I was caught in the middle, with my reputation and my client's loyalty at stake.

---

1. *Peter Principle*: In a hierarchy every employee tends to rise to his level of incompetence.—Laurence J. Peter
2. That company, a Fortune 500 in the 1970s, is now a mere skeleton of it's former self with only a couple of hundred employees and less than $10 million in annual revenues. Did these absurd, dishonest corporate policies have something to do with this corporation's demise?

Trying to be a good corporate politician without damaging my reputation or the company's relationship with the client, I endeavored to find a solution. Finally in a last-ditch move to protect my client relationship, I went to the Division President with my appeal. He had the clout and the ability to solve the problem. This was one of my hardest lessons about the *good old boys* network. He caved in and hid his head rather than enter into the fray and stand up for what was right. I was left alone dealing with a situation that threatened to compromise my integrity and jeopardize my career.

Then, one day when every company executive was coincidentally on an airplane, and conveniently out of touch, I received a phone call informing me that if my client did not pay his bill immediately, a truck would be sent to the bank's warehouse the next morning to reclaim our merchandise. I was stunned. This bank was doing well over $1 million a year in business with my company. At the time, 1981, $1 million certainly qualified the bank as a high value client.

My reputation and my company's relationship with this client were suddenly on the block. I remember the day as if it were yesterday. I was standing in a phone booth about five blocks from the client's office. I felt I had no choice. I was forced to a position of personal and professional vulnerability that I would have done anything to avoid.

I surrendered. I walked down the street and into the bank. On the long trip up the elevator, I wondered why this had happened. I second-guessed myself, trying to see where I had made the mistake. There was no answer. I felt certain that I would lose this client.

The client was in his office and he welcomed my unannounced visit. I sat down in his office and told him the whole tale. I hid nothing. I tried to hold back the tears of embarrassment and disappointment. But I could not. I cried (an unprofessional, but human thing to do). He was dismayed by the turn of events, but said he knew that I had been honorable and he would certainly be needing the products, so he would write me a check. While I waited, he wrote a check for about $400,000.00. He signed it and handed it across the desk, not because of the tears—because of the power of honesty and truth.

In succumbing to the truth and my own vulnerability, the problem was solved. The bigger part of this lesson was in the years to come, my business relationship with this man flourished as never before. When he moved on to another bank, he called me as soon as he needed my company's products and services. He referred other clients to me. He introduced me to some of his employees and I became a mentor to them. Until the day he retired, he trusted me and never left me for the competition. He helped me when I started a new venture, and because of relationships like this, I never doubted the value of being honest again.

Corporate culture would have us believe that there is a different standard for honesty in business life. A lesser or more manipulative standard that involves professional polish and corporate ethics, which are somehow different from personal ethics. This is not true and this very idea is why companies and the people working in them can remain disheartened and dysfunctional.

The leadership in that Fortune 500 corporation demonstrated greed, egotism, and dishonesty to employees with these pressure driven tactics. As leaders they had a responsibility far greater than getting big padded bonuses, a responsibility of principles. They failed and eventually the company failed.

Living with Principles

In order to work with integrity, we must be honest—honest with others and honest with ourselves about who we are and what it takes to satisfy our individual soul's needs. We can then examine how the corporate path we've chosen for our soul's journey either fulfills or undermines those needs. Creating a written list can help. This list, which is different for each of us, contains our basic requirements for peaceful and healthy survival.

My personal list of soul-nurturing human needs includes:

- The need to be challenged.
- The need to be around positive people.
- The need to be loved unconditionally.
- The need to know myself honestly.
- The need to be introduced to and use my creative side.
- The need to learn to love others unconditionally.

My life, including my existence in the business world, must fulfill these basic needs for me to feel healthy and at peace. Before you go on reading this book, I encourage you to take the time to write down your own basic needs.

We each must identify our unique personal needs for ourselves and cultivate them in our business journey. If your needs are unclear to you, you can develop your list as you begin to apply some of the broader principles in this book.

To survive and grow as whole, happy human beings we must each go into our *soul-center* to search for the powerful eternal values and use them in our corporate life, whether we work in the boardroom or the mailroom.

Harmonizing with a Corporate Culture

As we seek to live lives of integrity, we also must come to terms with the reality that we live in a material world. We are all corporate co-dependents. Materialistic consumption, cutthroat competition, and financial profit fuel this powerful corporate force.

Profit-driven principles, material status symbols, and corporate culture dominate the world today. Corporate influence is now greater than the influence of any government, more powerful than any church or religion, and more pervasive than any other social influence.

As corporate influence increases and expands, it washes over every area of our existence. In the United States, we are affected by corporate culture in most everything we do. An HMO (Blue Shield, Blue Cross, Kaiser, Aetna, Medicare) dictates how our medical care is dispensed, our children's first jobs are at chain restaurants (Taco Bell, McDonald's, KFC), our psychiatrists are informed by corporate insurers (managed health care) about how they may treat our emotional problems, a priest carries the Word of God managed by the (corporate) church, professional sports teams entertain us, and we have cappuccino at the corner coffee shop (Starbucks) that we drive to in our Ford or Lexus SUV. The list goes on.

As human beings living in this corporately-created environment, we have two choices: we can rigidly resist its negative influences, wailing about the sin and injustices of the brutal, materialistic, cutthroat competition or we can find a peaceful, harmonious way to integrate our spiritual goals and principles with this culture.

Beyond the basic needs list you create for yourself, the five spiritual principles outlined in this text will help you find inner peace and serenity while achieving rewarding personal and professional goals. They will also be the hallmark for your career success. Applying these spiritual principles to your life will be the most important work you will ever undertake. It will help you clarify your personal values and goals, thereby guiding you to define all your future actions.

The Five Soul Survival Principles

1. Honesty: Opening the Door to Your Soul

2. Gratitude: Count Your Blessings

3. Courage: Owning Your Power to Choose

4. Perseverance: Hanging On in the Dark Times

5. Trust: Living in the Light of Divine Destiny

These principles run counter to the tools for success offered by many motivational gurus, but they are based on the abiding and ancient truth of all human existence. As such, they will bring not only peace, but also soaring success to your chosen vocation. Seek the peace these principles promise and success will be a natural outcome.

Introduction to the Five Soul Survival Principles

All of life is a spiritual process. Nothing you experience is wasted when you seek the lessons in it. Practicing the five *Soul Survival* principles will help you begin operating in the world from a spiritual perspective. Using these principles won't guarantee you a painless existence, but it will deliver a life with a purpose that is deeply meaningful to you.

Principle One—Honesty: Opening the Door to Your Soul

Being honest means seeing yourself in the world as clearly as possible. Once you examine and dispel the illusions you hold about yourself, you free yourself to live a more genuine life. Being honest about everything opens the door to the soul. Honesty means rediscovering your authentic self, thereby clearing your vision about what is true for you.

Honesty in dealing with others flows naturally from self-honesty. When you are clear about what is true for you, and you have a clear connection with your personal truth, you have easy access to what is right or wrong for you, making it simpler to act with integrity. Acting from your authentic self, you will know your personal bottom line, you will be aware of actions that are unacceptable to you.

Becoming authentic by staying open and vulnerable is the single most powerful tool for clearing the path toward spiritual growth and awareness. It took the devastation of personal crisis to get my attention and create an opening for the consciousness of this spiritual connection. It was only after I had exhausted all the possibilities I could think of—after I had essentially given up the battle—that I was truly willing to become authentic and hence accept divine guidance. Before my crisis, what I call my *abyss experience,* I thought I had to be strong to survive. I thought being strong meant I had to make it on my own, keep my troubles to myself, and keep up a good front. A crushing defeat taught me about the interior strength of my soul, humility, and the power of surrender.

Principle Two—Gratitude: Count Your Blessings

When you look at the events in your life as lessons, you can use them to guide you along your spiritual path. When you honestly scrutinize your life, you will see the patterns you have been living. The types of jobs you accept, the people you encounter, and the struggles you seem to face repeatedly, all offer guidance if you seek it. When you can see even your struggles for the lessons they've offered, the strengths they've honed in you, those struggles become blessings that can broaden your overall sense of purpose. Gratitude smoothes the rough edges of difficult experiences and transforms pain into healing awareness.

Principle Three—Courage: Owning Your Power to Choose

When you embrace your own power, you allow no one else to define you. You also learn to understand the difference between who you really are and what is happening around you. When you operate from your own power, you know that neither your boss nor your paycheck is your source of power. Your true power source comes from within and from trusting in the wisdom of divine destiny.

The courage to acknowledge your vulnerability to yourself and others is really what creates internal confidence and strength because doing so breaks down your self-made prison of fearful isolation and bonds you to others in honesty and compassion. Living your life with open acknowledgment of your vulnerabilities is an act of great courage. In the vast majority of situations, being open and vulnerable will bring you closer to colleagues and clients as it urges you along your divine path.

Principle Four—Perseverance: Hanging On in the Dark Times

Perseverance is simply faith by doing. You can begin the practice of perseverance by being there for yourself every single day. Drawing on your willingness to see the lessons in life, you can learn to trust in long-term positive outcomes. When I was the victim of sexual abuse at the hands of a therapist, it was hard to see how that might benefit my career, but when the pain of this event erupted and I persevered in the belief that there is good in everything, I was blessed with a new inner strength that was a direct result of the abuse itself. When you persevere, you move yourself into the flow of miracles in action. When you are taking action in your own behalf, you are open to the opportunities and the 'chance meetings' that flow along your divine path. Persevering and trusting divine destiny gets you to where you are meant to go.

Principle Five—Trust: Living the Light of Divine Destiny

Divine destiny is what you make of it. Life offers you choices. You can choose to stumble blindly along your path, feeling battered by life's unpredictable ways, or you can open your eyes and heart, choosing to see more clearly. As you incorporate the five principles into your way of approaching life, your spiritual vision sharpens, and you will be able to see further along your divine path. As you learn your life lessons and act from internally-guided integrity, you will avoid many of the wrong turns along the spiritual path so lovingly prepared for you. And, as you travel toward your divine destiny you will discover that the journey toward the destiny is the destiny itself.

When you have an understanding of these principles and put them to work in your life, they become magically enmeshed into a single guiding force for success, and most importantly, spiritual peace. Divine destiny is not a place, it is a path.

These ancient principles, tried-and-true, will not guarantee a painless, joy-filled life. That is not a real life. There will be pain-a-plenty in your *life journey* but practicing these five principles is the soothing balm for all human pain.

3

Principle One—Honesty:
Opening the Door to Your Soul

Spiritual honesty and understanding will produce abundant professional confidence. It is easy in the day-to-day working world to be seduced into the corporate line or what others might consider just a normal business strategy. Honesty demands courage and rigorous self-analysis, but the pay off is the creation of a solid foundation for success.

April 30, 1996—This was one of those days when I was faced with my fearful, black self again and I wasn't too happy with the image. In the previous two years, my business had been successful and wonderfully exciting for the most part, but I worked in a highly technical industry and it was not without its challenges.

I struggled with lifelong learning disabilities, making it extremely difficult for me to absorb minutely detailed technological information. My industry had recently adopted a certification program. Individuals passing the test received Certificates of Competency.

Since I had founded the biggest training company in the industry, it made sense for me to incorporate this technical agenda into my training programs. I began reading every piece of technical material I could get my hands on. I sought out my technically-oriented associates to pry what I could out of their knowledge banks. It still was difficult for me to comprehend.

I was one of the first to take the pilot version of this new certification test. To my horror, I didn't pass. My confidence deeply shaken, I was flooded by memories of high school hurdles and failures. These were the hurdles I had run from to hide my incompetence from the world.

I was deeply embarrassed to tell people about my failure. It was like a return to the nightmare of my early desperate insecurities and fears. On my darker days, I imagined my whole business failing, because I couldn't seem to absorb this information.

I redoubled my study efforts and continued to integrate everything I learned into my training program. I took the test again. I failed. My frustration and fear grew, but I continued studying. I contracted with some hard-core *techies*, both to teach me and to help me incorporate the new material into my training program. One more time I took the test and once again, I failed.

My self-confidence was being tested to a new depth. I was furious with myself, frustrated beyond reason. After I failed the third time by only two points, I was crazed. I wanted to retake the test immediately. It was rescheduled for the same afternoon. Even though it cost $165 each time I took the test, I persisted. I refused to give up, and finally, at the fourth sitting, I passed. I was jubilant to have the certification at last, but at the same time, I feared that if people realized how hard it had been for me to absorb this technical data they would never entertain coming to my training classes. So I kept quiet about my struggle. After all, I was widely accepted as an expert in the industry. I remained silent as my peers bragged about their certification and compared their scores on the test.

I plowed ahead. My business and reputation soared. I kept my secret. After all, whose business was it anyway? No one needed to know. I wasn't breaking any rules by not telling. But this little dishonesty began chipping away at my heart. The corporate world is filled with exaggerations and omissions at every level, I reassured myself. This was no big deal.

But as fate would have it, my struggles with the certification test came to light with one of my larger clients. In a committee meeting discussing the test and what competency level was being addressed within it, it was revealed (to my dismay) that an industry expert and 20 year veteran (me) had required four tries to succeed. I was humiliated and embarrassed. The familiar feelings of inadequacy and fear immediately arose within me. I was faced with a choice to go on trying to conceal the struggle and put on the typical phony, corporate camouflage, or to just face facts and see what the lesson of truth-telling had to teach me. Acceptance is always the first step toward learning spiritual lessons. Still, I was filled with the old fears of inadequacy, rejection, and failure. I was sure I would lose the client and maybe many more clients. I sank into a deep depression.

Seeking comfort and validation for this little lie and corporate game-playing, I confided in a close friend. She pointed out to me a whole different side of this episode and, by the grace of some new awareness, I was able to hear her point. My awareness didn't make the struggle any easier, but it did allow me to handle it differently. She pointed out to me that the overriding message I am here to teach is the importance of perseverance and self-honesty in the business world. *Not* passing the test three times was not the important lesson. The lesson was illustrated by my going back a fourth time to try again. *I did not give up.* Only by failing three times did I get the incredible satisfaction of finally passing. My repeated efforts and eventual success helped me to acknowledge the gifts perseverance brings me in my personal and professional life. There is no certification test for honesty and perseverance. These are strengths of the spirit.

The technical training that I went on to deliver was sensitive to the spirits of all my class participants; sensitive to the learning struggles of some and the fears of others. I would begin my class by making it known that it took me three failures before I passed. Everyone in the class seemed to let down barriers a bit when they heard this and a more authentic learning experience was enjoyed by the entire class. The training I delivered encompassed more than preparation for certification. Although certification was important, nurturing the human spirit was far more valuable. The glory of who the participants were and what they could do in their chosen corporate careers was paramount. Communicating a sense of hope and purpose to each person in my class was the most rewarding work I've ever done.

WE TEACH BEST THE LESSONS
THAT WERE THE HARDEST FOR US TO LEARN.

I learned another lesson on this most important principle of honesty as I was forced to deal with my alcoholism in the midst of my fledgling career. I had been employed four years at the prestigious Fortune 500 company where my career began. Those four years were a struggle. I was young and completely enamored with corporate life, loving working in a man's world, and happy with my small successes. I had fallen right into the happy-hour office crowd. I was no stranger to the two-martini lunches popular in the seventies. I loved the corporate lifestyle, but I was the child of an alcoholic and my alcoholism had come into its own. I was on the way to complete devastation when I finally hooked up with people who could help me.

This incredibly difficult self-revelation spearheaded my success in that corporation for the next eight years. This lesson taught me that we are all human and because my boss and co-workers knew that I was a recovering alcoholic, I was blessed with opportunities to help others in the company. It is important to honestly and humbly expose who I am to everyone I meet. I am just a small human being living in a very big world and I am here only for a short time.

Corporate camouflage has been a corrosive force in my life. It has built walls of isolation around me. It does the same to so many others. To tear down those walls, I strive to reveal my strengths and vulnerabilities to the people I meet during my corporate adventures. I try not to hide my fears and insecurities. The amazing thing about this strategy of honest self-revelation is that so many people seem to experience a sense of new spiritual freedom when I speak of the kinds of vulnerabilities they themselves have been hiding for so long. We hide these things because we are afraid that if we let down our barriers for a single second, we will be buried in the corporate onslaught. My experience has been just the opposite. When I finally faced up to the weak and negative sides of my corporate persona, I discovered incredible new strength and great success. Only through this humbling acceptance did I have the courage to move forward toward my dreams. My dreams have been coming true. The truth really does set us free.

We are fragile, imperfect, and vulnerable human beings, all striving for a sense of peace and accomplishment. We have so many mistaken ideas about the source of that peace. What we know as the typical corporate ladder doesn't lead to spiritual peace. Those exhilarating experiences of achievement and accomplishment are like the temporary highs of drug addiction. The sturdy upward-bound rungs of spiritual growth are made of surrender, humility, and self-honesty.

What is Honesty?

Honesty isn't limited to *not lying*. It means seeing ourselves in the world as clearly as possible. In order for our divine destiny to reveal and fulfill itself, we must free ourselves from the illusions we hold about ourselves. Self-illusions develop in us from a very early age. Our parents begin defining who they think we should be from birth. Society reinforces widely held beliefs that deem us 'good' or 'bad', worthy or unworthy. In the United States, for example, the more material wealth we accumulate, the more we are valued as people. Television delivers an unattainable standard for beauty and advertising in all its forms, assures us that who we are is what we own. A big part of self-honesty is separating what everyone else says we should be from who we really are. Honesty with ourselves is the first step toward seeing our divine purpose with clarity. Once we examine and dispel illusions we hold about ourselves, we free ourselves to live a more genuine life.

IF YOU ARE NOT LIVING A LIFE GUIDED BY RIGOROUS HONESTY, THEN YOUR HIGHEST DIVINE DESTINY WILL GO UNREALIZED. BEING HONEST *ABOUT EVERYTHING* OPENS THE DOOR TO THE SOUL AND DEVELOPS SPIRITUAL COURAGE.

Honesty is rediscovering our authentic selves, thereby clearing our vision about what is true for us, and in business, what constitutes right action for us. Once we know who we are, our business and personal decisions will be based on an integrity most of us lost touch with at a very young age. The process of reconnecting with our souls—which is where our sense of authenticity resides—involves examining the childhood experiences and life events that shaped our current beliefs about ourselves. Though painful, even for those of us who lived very happy childhoods, this honest self-examination helps us recognize and strip away many of the false beliefs we hold about ourselves; self-illusions that separate us from connection to the natural guidance system of our soul.

Honesty in dealing with others grows naturally from self-honesty. When we are clear about what is true for ourselves and we have a clear connection with our personal truth, we have easy access to what is right or wrong for us, making it simpler to act with integrity. Acting from our authentic selves, we will know our personal bottom line, we will be aware of actions that are unacceptable to us. We will be able to pick our battles and "shoot from the heart" with confidence and courage.

Honest Self-Appraisal of the Past Frees us to Move Ahead

The first step for corporate success and personal peace is to be honest with yourself. I realize now that honesty is essential to long-term success. What you lie to yourself about or avoid because it's too unpleasant ultimately can sink your career. It almost sank mine. When I entered the corporate world, I was ashamed of my family and of my lack of education. Out of shame, I lied and misled others about who I was. As long as I did that, I was weak and ineffective. I was confused about who I was and what I wanted in life. My goals and desires were all tangled up with my parents' ideas and the coping behaviors I had learned during my early family life. Cover-ups and crazy pretending diluted my personal power. Being honest with and about myself seemed to demand more of me than I could deliver. I was afraid and I drank both to avoid the truth and to ease my fear of it.

The business of being honest with myself began as painful family secrets unraveled around me. Practicing honesty has been a powerful lesson and is a continuing challenge, but it has been well worth the effort. Looking closely at the people and events in my life has freed me from destructive patterns and revealed personal strengths that otherwise would have gone unrecognized. Practicing this unsparing self-honesty has uncovered and defined the excuses that would sabotage my success.

Growing up in a less than a privileged environment, I was the product of a broken and alcoholic home. Nurturing was a luxury experienced by stable and secure families, not my beleaguered group. My earliest feelings were of being afraid and being different. Verbal violence and emotional neglect characterizes most of my childhood. Between my father's heavy drinking and my mother's chronic fear, I lived in edgy anticipation of violent fights. I was terrified of being abandoned and I tried my best to keep my parents happy; a big job for a little kid. The situation never felt safe enough for me to let my own anger surface.

Our family had no white-collar role models. Money was very tight. There was always food on the table but we also were reminded that we were lucky to have it and that it might not be there tomorrow. As the oldest of three children, I took on a perceived leadership responsibility for my sister (who was four years younger) and brother (who was six years younger). If this wasn't enough, I shouldered the burden of my unhappy parents as well. In my heart, I believed that my very birth was the true cause of their misery. I felt that if I could just be good (and invisible) enough, then everything would be fine. I spent my whole childhood worrying about my parent's problems. I had no life of my own and no opportunity to find out who I was. I couldn't relax and explore my purpose or potential. I needed to be on the alert for potential life-threatening explosions or possible abandonment.

As children, human beings are completely dependent on their parents for food, shelter, and their view of the world. We grasp and define our world through our parents' beliefs. As my ideas developed, my mother's input was strongest. Her Depression era credo was this simple chant: *work and worry.* In my child mind, I defined good people as the ones who worked and worried. In my adult struggles to become the best person I could, I suffered great pain by unconsciously trying to live by this motto. I never really knew why, but I always felt that I should be working harder and I was always worried about the future. In learning to be honest with myself, I was able to expose these inner mantras. I was able to identify that the mantra was my mother's, not mine. Not until then could I let it go.

Examining childhood issues helps you first to identify them. Once you understand their origins, you will often better understand your motivations. You may well experience an *ah-ha* about that knee-jerk reaction that never made sense before you looked at your life and yourself in depth and with honesty. You may continue to react strongly in certain situations, but those reactions will no longer drive you blindly. You will know what you are doing.

You can also use this new knowledge to help consciously separate your past from your present. When you bring your old assumptions into your awareness, you may begin to recognize thoughts and behaviors that served you well when you were 10 or 20, but may scuttle your progress at 30 or 40. Once you see that your outmoded beliefs and behaviors are remnants from the past, you can decide which are yours, which are your family members', which ones you want to keep and which to discard.

Understanding old messages and past wounds helps you realize that as children, you may not have had a choice about your actions and responses in difficult situations, but as an adult, you have the power to choose. You can choose to respond differently now. Knowing what fuels your emotional responses at work and recognizing that you have the power to choose can be incredibly freeing.

Taking a close look at yourself, including successes and failures, strengths and shortcomings, can help you use the events in your life like markers on a map leading to genuine personal peace and prosperity.

Honest Self Appraisal Introduces You To Who You Are

I grew up in an atmosphere of conditional love not unlike today's corporate environment. If I got good grades, I got positive attention. If I got poor grades I got negative attention. But I only seemed to count when I was either producing or making trouble. The simple miracle of my existence counted for nothing. So I became a producer (and sometimes a troublemaker). The point is that my identity was built on what I did, not who I was. I learned to value myself for what I could do, never for who I was. My soul, the very essence of who I was, remained buried beneath layers of fear.

Today's corporate family is not much different. There may not be alcoholism and drug addiction as in mine, but often there is a lack of involvement with children's feelings and issues. We raise children today as if they were commodities. We get them to soccer and football and ballet, but we don't have the time to sit down, have a meal with them, and discuss their feelings, their fears, their dreams, and their other emotions. Many of us believe that if we put them in all of the right schools and activities, they will grow up to be the 'perfect' people (like products of a corporation). But what kind of people will they be? What kind of condition will we leave them in as spiritual beings with fears, dreams, emotions, and fragile self-esteems? With the corporate consciousness driving all couples to have two jobs, two cars, two televisions, etc., kids are shuffled into the corporate care-giving systems: day care and private schools. All these systems may be good, but the fast-paced life tells us to pay attention to building the bridges of unconditional love and acceptance for our children to connect with their inner soul guide.

When our work is clearly more important than our children's day-to-day issues, children feel unimportant. If Mom and Dad never listen, when they ask their child a question and then are distracted by their own work issues, this is evident to the child. Children learn to hold everything inside, including seething anger. Unfortunately, these children will likely grow into the same kinds of parents. Their hearts and souls know they have been shortchanged. And the underlying anger about this loss never gets vented. Instead, it leaks slowly from generation to generation until somebody blows his own head off or silently drinks herself blind.

Conditional love damages the soul. Every one of us needs to know that even when we are doing nothing at all; we are valued, we are loved. When children experience conditional love, approval hinges on their achievements. In their own hearts, achievement displaces their sense of connection to their souls. The core of their self-worth begins to build on external standards: how well they are doing in school, what brands of clothing they wear, how they compare to other kids, and later, how much money they make at work. These external standards can be quite alluring because they look so real. There are almost always people around us to judge how we measure up. There are grades, scales, and norms. We feel like we know who we are when we judge ourselves and live by these external standards. But what happens when things go bad? (They always do eventually.) What happens when we fail or lose our jobs or get fat or have skills and talents that fall outside the norms?

We all need unconditional love—the love that reminds us that we are precious spiritual beings at our core. When we begin to see unconditional love as a sacred and precious attribute, we will give it more freely. Built into unconditional love is self-compassion that reassures us, forgives us, and encourages us to try again even when the world judges us harshly. Even though we may not have experienced that kind of love in our lives before, we can start practicing it now. Even though we may not expect to receive it in our current corporate structure, we can *give* it there.

Once we begin giving unconditional love regularly, we begin to transform ourselves and our workplace. As more of us learn to love, even at work—especially at work—others learn to receive love and eventually to practice it themselves. As we learn to work from our souls, we give without resentment, we work together, and we feel free to use our authentic gifts. We benefit because we are working from a place of power and joy and the business benefits because we are giving it the best of ourselves.

Conditional Love and an Atypical Kid

My mother, from the very beginning, tried to provide me with the social and cultural accouterments of the day, but all of her well-intended choices (piano, ballet, tap dance) were so tedious and repetitive for me that they were unbearable. Those early failures loomed over me for years. I seriously believed I was an inferior person because of my inability to stick with these highly monotonous endeavors.

Our modern day educational system does not always help people to use their own brains, to think things out, and develop their own unique and creative conclusions. Looking back through history, the truly great thinkers and achievers of all time have not necessarily been the supremely educated, but they have always been people who could think for themselves, who trusted their own judgment, who took risks, and who constantly tried to draw their own conclusions.

My own education and my interest in it, was short circuited in my teen years. As I entered the more trying and taxing courses in high school, I was unable to perform. Although I was a marked overachiever in other areas, when the classes began to include serious detail and monotonous recurrent thinking, such as bookkeeping, algebra, Spanish, and geometry; I lost interest. Looking back and by today's understanding of disabilities, I had a learning disorder, ADD (*Attention Deficit Disorder*), and was unable to withstand day-to-day tedious educational pursuits. (My younger son was later diagnosed with this same disorder.)

My mind was quick and curious (appreciated as an ability for 'multi-tasking' in a high-tech world), but not at all suited to the formal, repetitive, and focused educational model. At first, I scraped by. As a born salesperson, I convinced my algebra teacher to give me a passing grade even though I had not absorbed anything about algebra. But this collapsed on me the next year when plane geometry was a requirement. Without algebra, I didn't have a prayer.

Bookkeeping came next. This was worse yet. I could not force myself to sit through that tedious class. I was failing and I felt like a failure.

Never a Secretary

My formal education experience became even more disastrous when my good and hard-working mother tried to instill in me the importance of learning secretarial skills. With passion and fervor she extolled the critical importance of learning these vital skills. She told me that as a woman, it would be my only chance for survival. Being a terrified soul already, I heard her message loud and clear. That message was one of a basic survival instinct. If I could not do these things, I believed I would literally starve to death. My fear was paralyzing.

Unfortunately, knowing nothing about ADD (*Attention Deficit Disorder*) I only knew I did not possess the ability to learn typing. It was as if there was a physical block between my brain and my fingers. As hard as I tried, the messages from my brain could not drive the fingers to the right keys on the typewriter with any consistency. I felt stupid and inadequate. My soul, my inner essence, was shriveling.

The problem escalated when my mother insisted that along with mastering the typing skills, that if I really wanted any success at all beyond just being another typist in the corporate typing pool, I must also learn the skill of shorthand. Shorthand was the ultimate educational crusher for me. After one week in the Shorthand Class, it was crystal clear to me that I would never be able to do this. There was no part of my brain or intellect that could possibly identify strange little squiggles and relate them to English words. I dropped out of the class and soon thereafter I dropped out of high school altogether. I felt like a terrible failure. My insecurity was as big as a house and my fear was a deep down fear of starvation and disaster.

My mother's skills were not passed on to me. I clearly was unable to follow in her footsteps. It seemed that my mother would be the only success and survivor in the family. She was the only person in the family with talents to strive toward. I could not measure up. Trying to achieve her kind of success made me feel like a failure. Without the unconditional love I needed to encourage me to explore my own individual strengths, I was at a loss to determine what to do with my life.

Early Perseverance and Learning to Work

I did have early, though modest, success in the world of work. In retrospect, these early successes probably saved what was left of my shaky self-esteem.

My career in sales began in 1954. At the age of ten and on my own, I began a door-to-door Christmas card business. The first money I made felt meteoric to me. I reveled in the independence borne of that first jingle in my pocket. This experience and my reaction to it were early signs of a corporate superachiever.

My first 'mainstream' job was in food services. (I was already looking at things from a corporate perspective.) At fourteen, I got a job as a carhop in a drive-in restaurant. My mother, struggling alone to raise three children, encouraged me to get a job and suggested that lying about my age might even be permissible in this case. I did and I got the job. I was thrilled, but getting the job was not easy. I was insecure and afraid. When I applied, I was tongue-tied. My mother told me to go back the next day, that if the owner saw how persistent I was, he might hire me just to get me out of his hair. I returned daily until he finally gave in. I learned that perseverance pays off.

I've always been grateful for any opportunity to work. The first time I saw my name on a paycheck, it was as if it finally legitimized my existence. The name on my paycheck became who I was.

This attitude has made me a more achievement-oriented individual than the average corporate citizen. I've never felt I was owed a living. I was grateful when anyone wanted me. Certainly a symptom of low self-esteem, but the attitude produced good (over-achieving) work habits in me. I thought that true happiness and success would come from making something of myself. My family revered financial achievement, even though they never had much of it. *Making something of yourself* was clearly defined as financial achievement in my family system.

The need to pay my own way with dignity and independence overpowered my pride. To this day, I would rather work at a fast-food restaurant turning hamburgers than not work at all. The dignity and self-esteem of contributing enough to take care of myself has been a driving force in my life. It was also the beginning of the mightiest spiritual lessons of my entire corporate career. The lessons of work and perseverance—showing up and participating.

These two early job experiences said more about the kind of contribution I would make to a corporation than all of the formal educational degrees in the world. *My attitude and desire were defined.*

My third job was in a local drug store. Several employees there were college students. One girl, a zealous and intelligent college student, couldn't use the cash register. Every time she worked the register, the money would be off and the boss would be furious. Other seemingly, intelligent people had no clue about how to help customers. It baffled me. I envied and looked up to these young women because they were getting an education, yet I couldn't help noticing that I was learning faster and working more efficiently than any of them.

Life Lessons

Examining childhood issues can teach us what we already know about ourselves, but may have been long forgotten. Some of this knowledge may validate our love for our current career; some may lead us in new directions. Reviewing even unsavory chapters in our lives will reveal character strengths and life lessons we may never have considered. Childhood issues are especially useful when we remember that no part of our life is separate from our spiritual life. Viewed in this way, we can choose to see experiences and interactions of all kinds as lessons in life, as a school for our souls. As I look back now, I see the strengths I developed in some of my most difficult situations.

For much of my early career life I did not see the significance of the crucial lesson my mother bestowed upon me: *the simple lesson of work.*

THE MOST IMPORTANT LESSONS ARE HIDDEN
RIGHT BEFORE OUR EYES
UNTIL WE MAKE A CONSCIOUS EFFORT TO DISCOVER THEM.

The subtle power of these lessons is lost to our day-to-day survival or success frenzy. When my mother's feet were put to the fire, she did not sit around watching daytime television bemoaning her awful fate. With my father in prison and three children to feed, she went to work. Important lessons in life are the simple ones demonstrated to us in the actions of others.

In a round about way, my father started a life lesson that taught me that I am worth more than my sexuality. He was a Merchant Marine and an interminable world wanderer. He lacked the stable temperament of more typical fathers and husbands. He seemed to me much like a good-natured hobo with a heart as big as the ocean. He was always bringing home stray animals and people, and despite his wandering ways and heavy drinking, I loved him dearly.

When I was eleven years old, my father disappeared from my life completely. In my experience, he had abandoned me. I was confused and alone. No one told me where he had gone or when he was coming back. He was simply gone. I lived in a family of secrets. Only 20 years later did I discover that he had been imprisoned for writing bad checks. Had I known he was *unable* to return, and that my actions had nothing to do with his disappearance, I wouldn't have felt so personally abandoned. Honesty about the situation would have minimized the damage. As it was, I ached for a loving male in my life.

Only much later in therapy did I learn about the importance of a father to a daughter in puberty. Fathers play a crucial role by reflecting a pure, non-sexualized sense of wholeness and self-esteem to their young daughters as they mature into women. Without that purity reflected back to me, I saw much of my worth as sexual. As a woman who would enter the predominantly male corporate arena, I was seriously and blindly disabled. I was at sexual risk with male authorities and some took full advantage of my vulnerability, until I learned that my contributions were valuable and that I did not have to trade my sexuality for a chance at success. From the soul lesson perspective, my father's absence, and my response to it, *eventually* taught me that I was worth more than my sexuality.

My father was an open and loving man who lacked skills, ambition, and education. He set no work ethic example for me, but he did teach me never to judge another human being. Until you've walked in another person's shoes, until you've lived in his skin, you cannot know what that person is about.

My father was also an alcoholic. As time passed I followed his lead and danced his dance. The lessons his presence—and his absence—set into motion in my life were some of the toughest and most valuable of all.

I NEVER MET A MAN I DIDN'T LIKE.
TRY THE SHOES ON THAT ARE HIS,
FEEL WHAT MAKES HIM WHAT HE IS,

WHAT IT'S LIKE INSIDE HIS SKIN,
LIVING IN THE SKIN HE'S IN,
JUST LIKE ME A LUMP OF SOD,
THERE BUT FOR THE GRACE OF GOD...
Credo—Will Rogers 1879–1935

Marry Well or Learn to Type

By the time I was seventeen, I believed that my only choices for happiness lay in mastering secretarial skills or marrying well. Restless and filled with fear, I married. I thought I was marrying well, but I really expected my husband to save me from the scary path ahead. I needed a protector and a savior. I doubt he had any idea what he was getting into with me. I had no idea myself.

The man I married came from an upper middle class family. His father worked for a well-established corporation. His mother never worked out of the home. Their life was the picture perfect vision of the way I thought life should be. I believed that the son would follow in his father's footsteps and I would be magically lifted from my unhappy background. I reinforced that fantasy by having two children right away. By the time I was 21, I was the uneducated, unskilled mother of two.

The man I believed would free me from my background had turned out to be less than ambitious. Worse still, he was a compulsive gambler. On many occasions during our seven-year marriage, I struggled to feed our family. At a very low point during this discouraging partnership, I mixed Bisquick with water to cook up doughy carbohydrate dinners. It was the only meal I could provide when we didn't have enough money to go to the market.

By convincing my husband to join the Navy I was finally able to receive a $90-per-month allotment check; money my husband couldn't get into his gambling hands. At least I could put food on the table. Following the fleet, we lived in converted, army-green WW2 warehouses in Virginia. They were infested with cockroaches, not fit for decent human inhabitants. When I brought my first child home from the hospital to this dismal place, I found cockroaches in his bed. It sickened me, but I felt hopelessly trapped. There was nowhere to turn.

I toughened up during this time. I learned to buy enough food to feed three people for two weeks on $27. When I later returned to the West Coast, friends asked why I never went to see our nation's capitol. We didn't have the money to buy gas.

I share the dubious beginnings of my adult life here because they illustrate how we can blindly stumble along, weighed down by so many false ideas about who we truly are. Yet when I take the high view—the soul lesson view of this period—I realize that it laid the groundwork for a serious desire to learn more about my *life purpose:* to find spiritual strength and to rise out of a living hell that I had clearly, though unconsciously, chosen for myself. I learned that I did have the strength to survive in extremely poor conditions, and perhaps most importantly, I learned that I had the power to choose a different way.

The Corporate Soul Survival Lesson: Our Lives Are Not Mistakes!

What does this painful review of my young life have to do with spiritual living in the business world? All that I learned then has helped me to become who I am now. My business life is inseparable from my spiritual life. When I glean all the knowledge I can from my past, I can apply it to my present and future spiritual life. Moreover, reviewing life from a spiritual perspective helps to shine light on and to give meaning to some of my darkest days.

The persevering attitude and desire for decency I developed during my young life were the bedrock of my spiritual education. The business world sets great stock in formal education and although formal education is indeed important, true character building, wisdom, and success come from the innate talent and mental toughness in each of us. Attitude and desire weigh more heavily than education in determining corporate superstars. With maturity, we have the opportunity to change our attitudes in ways that will enhance our careers and lives. As human/spiritual beings seeking who we are meant to become, our true greatness is cultivated and developed by unconditional love and approval. As I said earlier, we cannot expect to receive this kind of love within the world of work as it exists. Instead, we must begin working from our own hearts, giving unconditional love, making it safe for others to work from their hearts as well.

The spirit of the business enterprise lies in the spiritual condition of its entire workforce. Strength of character, positive attitudes, mental toughness, and desire for success exist in strong corporate structures, but are often buried beneath performance, profit, and production priorities. Corporate success can be enhanced and achieved by those willing to practice the spiritual principles of greatness. Each employee of a corporation has the opportunity to take on the responsibility of leadership and this begins with leadership of your own soul-self.

Our lives are not mistakes. Human beings are primarily spiritual in nature. Intellectual power, educational power, and emotional power are insignificant in the light of spiritual power. Spiritual power is our belief in the gifts we have as unique individuals. Everyone has these gifts. Each of us is a powerful spirit. When we believe in the greatness and wisdom of our own spiritual power, we can relax and enjoy the journey of our destiny.

Nelson Mandela[1] exemplifies this spiritual power in his 1994 inaugural address (We were born to make manifest the glory of God that is within us.[2]). Spiritual power is the belief in one's own greatness, as well as a spiritual source beyond the self. Remember, you are great. Each of us is living out a pre-ordained destiny with his or her own greatness. Many of us become frightened and shut down. We begin to believe in the lies that tell us we're limited or inferior. No one is inferior. Each human life has a unique and special set of powerful spiritual tools. Look at your life. What have you learned so far? Look for the lessons. Look for your strengths and learn from both dark and light times.

Our spiritual journeys should acquaint us with our inner gifts, the talents that are uniquely ours. The people we meet and the lives we touch, cannot be fulfilled by any other spirits. Our family members, our friends, and most certainly, our co-workers, are our spiritual teachers. They also happen to be our spiritual students. When we view our business relationships as opportunities to teach and to learn spiritual lessons, we look at them with new respect. Our colleagues play significant roles in our own growth and development as spiritual beings.

However, seeing our colleagues as spiritual classmates does not mean we have to engage in destructive behaviors with those whose lives may be off-course. We do have the choice to remain or to leave. These difficult people

---

1. Nelson Mandela—Former President of South Africa and African National Congress
2. See a longer quote from the Nelson Mandela *1994 Inaugural Address* Chapter 5, Page 53.

could be here to teach us that we are finished with these kinds of relationships. On the other hand, we may be learning more about ourselves through their behavior and may choose to stay with them until we sense completion.

I once had a boss who was incredibly insecure. The only way he felt safe and content was when everyone in the office was pitted against one another. He used the tactics of competition and comparison to cast each person in a negative light. He lied about each person's performance and created an atmosphere of suspicious isolation. This man was an intensely unhappy person and from his position of power, he drew others into his misery with him. In the shadow of his negativity, many of us lost our own identity and unconsciously entered his manipulative fantasy. We had given over our own inner missions, the power of belief in ourselves, and our trust in a greater destiny.

As I look back with a spiritual eye, I see that this man was a teacher who helped me to see more of myself—to see the parts of myself that needed strengthening before I could feel strong and whole. Today, I would never choose to work with someone like that. I learned what I needed to learn, and then I moved on.

Co-workers can play all kinds of spiritual roles in our lives. We have the choice to learn or not to learn from them. We can detach or engage. We can think about who at work 'pushes our buttons' to discomfort or who makes us feel at ease. All of our reactions to the people around us reveal more about our spiritual nature. Only we know what we need or wish to learn and when we wish to move on.

How My Ignorance Served Me: When the Student Is Ready the Teacher Will Appear

I spent my young life vainly searching for someone else and to be someone else. First, I looked to another person to bring me peace and safety. Later, I looked to the corporation for security, peace, and prestige. But everywhere I went, there I was. I couldn't escape the sense of emptiness built into my fragile core.

The difficult and challenging experiences in our lives often teach the greatest lessons. My unstructured upbringing, instability, and the absence of white-collar role models in my life turned out to be blessings in disguise. As I moved into the business world, I was defenseless against a system I didn't understand. I was socially, spiritually, and corporately ignorant. I had no formal skills to prepare me for this new world. Because I felt I never truly 'fit in' in the first place, it was easy for me to see how the corporate environment needed to change so that I could fit in. It had always felt uncomfortable. I had never felt that I could be my authentic self and succeed. As a result, my life in the corporate world has been an adventure in discovering who I am and learning how I could contribute toward positive change.

When I see life as a spiritual school, I see that much of my educational time has been spent in the corporate classroom. They say, *when the student is ready the teacher will appear.* Many of my teachers have worn conservative suits and held fancy corporate titles. In fact, when I was ready, the right teacher has always appeared.

Living a life of rigorous honesty is not an easy path, but it is always the simplest and most rewarding choice. When that choice is made, obstacles melt into opportunities.

Practicing rigorous honesty will:

- Turn failures into victories.
- Connect you with your true self.
- Open you to your divine guidance.
- Bring you to your true life-path.
- Greatly simplify your decision-making process.

4

Principle Two—Gratitude: Count Your Blessings

Mid-Year 1976—Even though I was unaware of it at the time, my corporate life was offering me spiritual lessons from the very start. One of the first lessons was about the meaning of true blessings. My company had a reputation for grooming its executives to be future politicians. During my tenure, one of our executives was elected a US senator and another was tapped as a presidential aide. It was widely assumed that they had picked another future leader when they hired a new executive that I'll call Richard (not his real name). Richard had all 'the right stuff.' He had starred on his Ivy League football team while excelling academically. He had a picture-perfect family, a lovely estate, and the social visibility and charisma it takes to acquire political power. As expected, Richard quickly excelled in the executive hierarchy. By the time he entered his second year with us, he was a shining corporate role model and an exceptional team leader. From my vantage point, his life seemed truly blessed with all of the advantages I yearned for in my life. The news of his death stunned us all.

Apparently, Richard's thirteen-year-old son had come home from school to find his father lying in a pool of blood, the result of having put a shotgun in his mouth. The shock of this event drove home two powerful lessons: first, things aren't always what they seem, and second, the kinds of things the world typically counts as blessings aren't always the things that satisfy our souls.

Even though Richard appeared to have acquired all the ingredients for happiness, his death challenged my belief in the definition of blessings as 'the good things', such as wealth, vibrant health, and the approval of other people. Despite all his external blessings, Richard had despaired.

Although Richard's story is an extreme case of external appearances being out of alignment with internal reality, it is not particularly unusual. As human beings, our emotional struggles are largely the same, regardless of our socio-economic status. Once we admit that to ourselves and others, we almost instantaneously realize that we are not alone in our personal pain. When we take a closer look, we come to realize that pain *conceals* the blessings. So rather than deny our painful experiences and feelings, we can look for the lessons and the blessings they hold for us.

BLESSINGS ARE THE RESULT OF A FULL HEART
NOT A FULL BANK ACCOUNT.

Follow The Yellow Brick Road

As children, many of us were enthralled by Dorothy's plucky spirit in the movie, The Wizard Of Oz.[1] Symbolically, she embraced her sense of inade-quacy, pushing on in spite of feeling stupid, heartless, and cowardly. Driven by her need to find her way 'home', Dorothy overcame terrifying obstacles. In her struggles, she discovered that her internal Scarecrow did indeed have a brain. The act of thinking a problem through had revealed it. Likewise, her Lion found his courage by being forced to face fear and her Tin Man uncovered his loving heart during an act of loyalty under duress. Finally, when Dorothy squared off with the Wicked Witch of the West, it took only a bucket of water to dissolve the illusion of the witch's power. Dorothy showed us that we already possess the qualities we need to make us happy, and that through hon-

---

1.   *The Wizard of Oz*, Warner Bros. Studios, 1939

oring and facing the obstacles in our lives, we reveal the strength and luster of our souls.

I wouldn't omit a single event in my life. There were no mistakes. Each profoundly painful period has helped me chip away at my false self. Each revelation has brought me closer to my true self—my soul self. The more I have learned to see life's obstacles as blessings in disguise (sometimes in very good disguise!), the more I have learned from them.

Blessing #1—Living in a Dysfunctional Family

I grew up wild, much like a weed in the wind. In this dysfunctional setting, I did not understand the blessing concept. For a long time I felt abandoned about being raised that way, but now I can see what a benefit it has been for me not to have had a structured upbringing. Rather than taking structure for granted, as I would have, had it always supported my thinking, I learned about life through a lot of painful trial and error. Because I held fewer assumptions about structure, I had to pay close attention and I learned my lessons well.

Blessing #2—Living on Welfare

As a twenty-five year old mother of two young children, I found myself living on welfare. I suffered deep humiliation about having to depend upon the government and the charity of others to feed my children.

Usually, at this point in the success story, you will hear about how the woman on welfare enrolled in college, got a teaching degree, and went on to provide a good and stable life for herself and her children. I must have heard that story too, because that's exactly what I tried to do. My neighbors persuaded Catholic Charities to help us with food. I enrolled in a five-year teaching credential program at the local junior college. It was a disaster. I didn't make it through the first semester.

Even as an adult, I lacked the ability to sit quietly in a learning environment for an extended period of time. ADD (*Attention Deficit Disorder*) still limited my academic abilities. Five years in school seemed like an impossible request to make of myself. With two babies at home to feed and worries about rent, food, and basic necessities, I couldn't concentrate for more than five minutes at a time. I chastised myself once again for lacking determination and perseverance.

Soon after that, I was informed that even with a degree, I might not make enough money to pay for daycare and living expenses for two small children.

This was the perfect excuse for me to quit the formal educational process once again and strike out to survive some other way. I continued searching for a way off welfare but I was terrified that I might not be able to make it on my own with two children.

I knew I couldn't go to work in the typical 'female 9 to 5' environment and ever make enough money to feed three hungry people. Besides, beneath my fear I yearned for a better life. Equipped with my father's lessons about the equality of all people and my mother's lessons about the value of common sense, I doggedly pursued a job where someone would give me a chance. I searched for a job in which I could excel if I worked hard enough.

A Note About Welfare

Getting off of welfare and finding an opportunity in the corporate system is not as simple as many may think. Most of us coming off welfare face tremendous dysfunction at every turn. It trips us up and sends us tumbling back into dependence. People entering a new world of independence need role models who have been there and know that it can be done. Single mothers holding down jobs for the first time need to know that they do have talent and value. But first they need to learn the skills of surviving day-to-day work life and meeting employer expectations.

The second step for them is to begin to see the greater self within themselves. If they have never seen that greater person within, if no one ever reflected their inherent value back to them, then it can be pretty hard for them to even glimpse, much less believe in. If they have come from a severely dysfunctional family, as I did, it may take years of therapy and mistakes before they are able to see any meaning at all behind life's obstacles.

Being a welfare mother was so intolerable for me that it drove me to find good work, to seek a better road for my children and myself. My determination to pull myself out of poverty taught me the importance and effectiveness of showing up for myself every day.

Blessing #3—Affirmative Action

My job search was built on blind perseverance, sheer desperation, and extreme frustration. I adopted a routine of going into one employment agency after another. They would pull out the little job box. (In 1969, before computer listings, available jobs were listed on 3" x 5" cards kept in little tin recipe boxes.) The agencies always had two boxes, one for men's jobs and the other for women's jobs. You can imagine what was in the women's box: *typing*. After awhile, I began suggesting that we forget the women's job box right off the bat.

"Let's look in the men's box. Maybe we can find something in there I can do," I'd suggest hopefully. Sure enough, we did come up with some possibilities. I went on some very strange interviews, but I found that most of the men's jobs held out the possibility for a well-defined career path.

After months of interviews, I was offered three different jobs in the same week. Two of the jobs paid more, but the third job intrigued me. Although it paid a lower salary, it held the promise of making unlimited income in commissions. I took that job. It was an entry-level sales position with a Fortune 500 corporation. Was it a fluke that I got this job? Not entirely, for there was fervor, perseverance, and intensity in my job search. I had two children to feed. I lacked skills and family support. *All I had was attitude and desire.*

I happened to be searching for work during the initial phase of the Affirmative Action movement. For the first time, regardless of sex or race, managers were being directed to diversify their ranks in different areas of their companies. I was told I had been hired because I was a woman. (This corporation was under pressure to bring gender and/or racial balance to its sales and marketing personnel). Whatever the circumstances were, I was elated at the opportunity.

I was hired to sell office equipment. Did I know anything about office equipment? I didn't know anything. I suspect the company anticipated that I would quickly fail. This job included hauling heavy machines into the field for customer demonstrations; certainly not a job for a 'weak little woman'. Physical strength would be the least of my problems. I figured I could always find a helpful man around and I did. I remember once resorting to buying a *wino* a bottle in payment for helping me unload a machine from my car. I did whatever was needed to get the job done. Unlike my male counterparts, I knew I was on trial. I might never get another chance like this. I knew there were those just waiting for me to prove that a woman couldn't do the job.

I entered into the corporate world with fear and insecurity, with optimism and excitement. I got my first corporate job through Affirmative Action and as my career developed, my company found that they had inadvertently hired a top producer.

When I was offered a rare and blessed opportunity to enter the corporate world with essentially no identifiable qualifications other than being female and having a positive attitude, I experienced early inklings of faith in a higher purpose for my life.

Blessing #4—Living a Corporate Life

The corporation was my version of the 'Great Kingdom of Oz.' Early on, I struggled to fit in and excel, despite my lack of preparation for a fast-paced professional sales position. I faced my fears, overcame many obstacles, and moved into the ranks of the top sales professionals. Getting there had seemed to be a great end in itself. Once I had arrived at the palace, however, I found that financial independence didn't provide me with a sense of personal fulfillment. Getting the job and learning the ropes, were the first steps on my 'Yellow Brick Road' to wholeness.

How I live my life today is no longer separate from how I make a living. My corporate life is intimately and intricately interwoven with my spiritual life. I go out the door in the morning excited about the adventure awaiting my career and my soul today. My corporate life is the pathway for my spirit to grow.

Blessing #5—Alcoholism and Addiction

My father left me the legacy of alcoholism. His father probably left him the same legacy. It has been my greatest blessing. I have been the first family member fortunate enough to find recovery.

Many recovering people say that the blessing *is* the recovery. This is true but if I search for the deeper spiritual lessons, the blessing is the addiction, the sickness, and the hopelessness of the illness. This disease is a *dark night of the soul* experience and the resulting spiritual growth has been my greatest gift. From this illness I learned the lessons of humility and surrender. Humility and surrender bring about a deep and abiding peace. Recognizing my weaknesses and vulnerability for the first time brought a transformation of my entire belief system. The blessing of this illness literally introduced me to God and educated me about my place in God's world.

I would not wish to go back and live through the terrors and loneliness of active alcoholism again. I'd certainly not wish it on anyone else, but the devastation of the disease taught me that good things always come out of bad things when experiences are viewed from a spiritual perspective. Out of my heartbreaking struggle to overcome alcoholism came strength of character I could have achieved only by passing through the doorway of pain.

Blessing #6—Motherhood

I've often said that I had children before I learned that I wasn't mother material. I was nineteen when I had my first son. In some cultures this is old for motherhood, however, I was a child myself, looking for someone to love and the yellow brick road to the Land of Oz.

Through the mistakes I made as a mother came the humility and honesty it took to connect with my children at the soul level. Being a mother stretched me from the inside out. I was forced to achieve more and be stronger than I would have been had I never had children. My relationship with my children today is forged from honesty and love. My children taught me about a mother's unconditional love. Today they are my greatest joy and the blessing is immense.

Blessing #7—Living with Fear

In 1995 I was on an airplane trip from California to Florida with my husband and my eldest son, Bob, who was 30 years old at the time. I noticed some tension in my son as we took off. Later during the flight he confessed to me his fear about flying and told me he was going to do something about it. I asked what he thought he could do. He said that he was going to try skydiving when he returned home. I was surprised and somewhat amused. I've tried to never let fear stand in the way of living my life. Maybe he inherited this tenacious spirit from me. He did go skydiving and fell in love the sport. Skydiving has become an important and fulfilling part of his divine destiny.

Facing paralyzing fear that had brought me to my knees and permeated every aspect of my life, has granted me the divine gift of courage. I have learned that I am never alone and that there is nothing real to fear. I learned to keep moving through my fear and never again let it stop my growth.

Blessing #8—Sexual Abuse

In my efforts to heal the wounds of sexual abuse, the profound pain that wrenched my heart also brought insights that were healing in nature. The pain had opened my heart to forgiveness and introduced me, once again, to God, the greatest healer of all. Above all, pain had equipped me with the unexpected gift of compassionate understanding for others and myself.

Learning to perceive overcoming obstacles in my life as opportunities to clear the pathway to my soul has brought me great peace of mind. In this sense, I see my obstacles as yet-to-be discovered blessings.

Turning Pain Around

They say there are only two things we can count on in life: death and taxes. If I may be so bold, I would add a third thing to that list. We can count on death, taxes, and *pain*. Pain is inevitable. Accordingly, the attitude we adopt about pain colors our perception of everything else that comes along in our lives. Success, joy, and freedom or defeat, despair, and isolation can be the result of our attitude about pain.

I am not an extraordinary human being. In fact, I am quite ordinary. The joy and success I've experienced is available to each of us. I don't possess exceptional talent and I certainly didn't have a privileged upbringing. It was my experiences of pain and fear that drove me to become more than I had ever hoped to be. The transformation of my attitude toward pain has become the touchstone for my spiritual progress.

Learning to seek spiritual meaning in life's difficulties has helped me maintain hope in some potentially devastating circumstances. My belief that failure and success are part of the same experience carries me through the unpleasant, but necessary failure part of the equation. We can learn to thank God for the failures. Each failure leads us one step closer to fulfillment and success.

April 1993, New York City—I found the courage to re-enter the business I had been weaned on. I was coming back from the second *abyss experience* of my career life. I had plunged downward as life seemed to heap on the pain: A very ill husband, a drawn-out lawsuit, as well as, an abusive boss had drained me. I had suffered a serious emotional breakdown. My greatest fear was that I would never be able to return to the business in which I had succeeded and excelled. But I managed to finagle a speaking slot on a panel at a New York technology exposition. I presented myself as an industry expert even though I had been gone for four long years. I was out of sync with the rhythm of the industry and I was fearful about my abilities to be onstage as an *expert*.

I showed up at the biggest convention center in the country, the *Javits Center*, with a presentation I had worried and slaved over for months. I was not very savvy technically and, although I'd figured out how to do the entire presentation on my little Macintosh PowerBook computer, I never realized that the Macintosh model I had, had no video outlet! There was no way for me to get the presentation out and on screen. Luckily, I did come prepared with overhead transparencies, which in the age of high-tech capabilities were sadly ineffective.

The *good* news was that I was only a small part of the panel, so I didn't bear all the responsibility for its performance. The *bad* news was that the panel (as a whole) got a poor rating: a black mark on my reentry. It had been a dismal failure. When I reapplied the next year they refused me a speaking slot.

By now, I had learned my soul lesson; in my life, failure frequently comes before success. Now I knew to just manage the failure and persevere. I reminded myself to go that extra mile—that success is just around the corner. What I can learn during the "bad" times helps me to create the good times.

Coming Back: Like a Rock Star

April 1995, Chicago—Two years later I was a featured speaker at that same Industry National Convention held in Chicago that year. I used my new state-of-the-art $6,000 laptop computer to support my presentation (a computer that my prospering business had purchased for me).

Just a month earlier this same new computer had failed me on stage in front of 300 people, but that time, unlike my New York experience in 1993, it had been all right because *I was all right*. I had grown. My fear was contained and managed in powerful and wonderful ways. I was able to take a deep breath, explain the technology failure to my audience, and do my presentation anyway. *What was my secret? My being was centered. What was the lesson? I am just another human being. I have only one essential message to share; it is the message of my life and my heart.* When I spoke before that audience, it may have sounded like I was talking about complex, high technology systems, but I was not really. With hearts listening, the audience heard about my humanity, their humanity, and the glory of our very existence on earth. They heard messages taught from my soul.

In Chicago, I had arrived for my presentation early. I was nervous. As I waited, I spotted a new friend in the audience. To relieve my jitters, I went down to talk with her.

During my preparation, I had found that all of my fancy new computer equipment seemed to be working this time. I was infinitely grateful when my presentation appeared, like magic, on two monstrous screens that beamed out into the huge auditorium. My fear immediately spoke to me: *The slides looked better at home on my laptop's miniature screen.* My soul stepped in: *Quit picking on yourself, Lynne. Ask God to help.*

Then I was on. It felt good when I started talking. I relaxed. I introduced myself. I told my audience what I wanted them to get from my talk: tools that would give them confidence when they went back to implement new high-tech systems in their companies. I appeared to be talking technology, but really the subject was the unflagging human spirit, the hidden reservoir of greatness in each of us, and the issues involved in doing our jobs in our chosen fields with a loving human touch.

Suddenly there was not enough time. *Talk faster Lynne,* my fear insisted. (My fear will always coach me to have more material than I need so I'm not left standing in front of everyone with nothing left to say.) But that day, my timing was perfect. The last slide illustrated the final point I wanted to make. The lights came up, and the doors opened to release the audience. *Hooray! I made it. Wait...*

Instead of streaming out the door, people swarmed to the front, grabbing and churning to get copies of my handouts. They told me they thought my presentation was great. When I ran out of handouts, it seemed like they were going to riot. I felt like a rock star. I told them to give me their cards; I would send the materials. Cards were piling onto the table. People wanted to discuss their cases with me, too many people. The next speaker was trying to set up and he wanted us out of the way. All day long, people who had been in the audience approached me. They told me they appreciated my talk and my style. I was elated.

Still floating from the pleasure of having reached so many people with my talk, I headed to the bookstore to see how my book on motivational sales was doing. This book was borne of my sales experience and the power of my new computer. Most of it just flowed out of me, and over a period of two years, with the help of many others, I had produced one of the most comprehensive sales and technical training manuals in the industry. The bookstore had made a conservative purchase of 10 copies. After all, it was new and at $125 apiece, the books were not cheap, and their price would increase to $295 after the introductory offer.

I couldn't find any of my books when I arrived at the bookstore. *Where did they put the sample copy?* I wondered. I knew they had more in a box some-where. I began fretting; *how could anyone buy it if they didn't know it's there?* Finally, I located the store manager, a nice woman named Lisa.

"Where are my books?" I asked.

"Oh," said Lisa, "they've been sold out since 3:00 P.M. on opening day."

"What?" I was stunned. "Well, where's the sample?"

"I had to sell the sample," she apologized. "Someone insisted."

I was overwhelmed. I put my last copy out with firm orders not to sell it and included order forms to last the rest of the convention.

The high from that day kept me awake nearly all night. My legs ached from pounding the show floor. I awakened the next day red-eyed and blurry-brained. I had an important 8:00 A.M. meeting to start my day. I was to meet with a publisher and exposition planner who would be setting up the annual New York Exposition in the Fall. They wanted me to be a keynote speaker at the conference. The meeting went very well. I was asked to contribute a feature piece for the fall show.

As the show wound down, I saw new and old friends and associates, people who spent large portions of their lives involved in a sterile technical milieu, people who were challenged to bring meaning and purpose to the day-to-day dealings of the technology workplace.

A footnote: The *Unibomber* was arrested that same day. This man claimed that technology would destroy the human race. How frightening to think such an alienated view was created out of the genius of mankind. As human beings with careers in the technology arena, we are constantly challenged to embrace impersonal technology and entwine it with the central purpose of human life, which is to love and care for one another. In my little sector of that technical world, I saw that happening over and over again. Technology can be, and often is, a gateway to rewarding and loving human relationships and experiences. Like anything else, how we use the gifts of our life and time determine our level of personal peace and joy.

The corporate *Soul Survival* lesson here: Failure and success go hand-in-hand. Savor sweetly the successes. Know that successes and failures are all part of the same experience.

CULTIVATE AN ATTITUDE OF GRATITUDE FOR EVERYTHING.

I learned that when I had an *attitude of gratitude*, I was happy. I learned that gratitude was a choice I could make.

Back to the Land of Oz

Dorothy's visit to the Kingdom of Oz taught us so much about our journeys to our authentic selves, our *soul selves*. Dorothy gained great strength as she faced, embraced, and overcame the obstacles she encountered along the Yellow Brick Road. She thought she had reached the end of her journey when she saw the material splendor of the Kingdom of Oz. Yet, when it finally came to truly returning to herself, none of the Great Oz's smoke and mirrors could take her where she needed to go. She needed to do the work herself. Since all the support, admiration, and effort of the Land of Oz had failed to get her home, Dorothy looked inward once more, and gathered the strengths she had developed in her dramatic inner life adventure. Within an instant of realizing her inner power, she revealed to herself her greatest blessings, and that she needed only to look within once more to get there, she was home at last.

5

Principle Three—Courage: Owning Your Power to Choose

WHAT ARE WE SO AFRAID OF?
OUR DEEPEST FEAR IS NOT THAT WE ARE INADEQUATE.
OUR DEEPEST FEAR IS THAT WE ARE POWERFUL BEYOND MEASURE. IT
IS OUR LIGHT, NOT OUR DARKNESS THAT FRIGHTENS US. WE ASK OUR-
SELVES: "WHO AM I TO BE BRILLIANT, GORGEOUS, TALENTED, AND
FABULOUS?"
ACTUALLY, WHO ARE YOU NOT TO BE? YOU ARE A CHILD OF GOD.
YOUR PLAYING SMALL DOESN'T SERVE THE WORLD. THERE IS NOTHING
ENLIGHTENED ABOUT SHRINKING SO THAT OTHER PEOPLE WON'T FEEL
INSECURE AROUND YOU. WE WERE BORN TO MAKE MANIFEST THE
GLORY OF GOD THAT IS WITHIN US.
IT'S NOT JUST IN SOME OF US; IT'S IN EVERYONE. AND, AS WE LET OUR
LIGHT SHINE, WE UNCONSCIOUSLY GIVE OTHER PEOPLE PERMISSION
TO DO THE SAME.
AS WE ARE LIBERATED FROM OUR OWN FEAR, OUR PRESENCE AUTO-
MATICALLY LIBERATES OTHERS.
NELSON MANDELA-INAUGURAL ADDRESS 1994

Why are we so afraid to shine? I believe that most of us can sense the wisdom in Nelson Mandela's words. We know we each have something unique to
offer. What holds us back from offering our talents to the world? I believe that
our hesitation stems largely from one or both of two primary fears. The first is
the fear that the genuine, precious, and very vulnerable gifts we offer will be
soundly rejected. What will be left of us once 'they' have rejected the most
cherished parts of ourselves? Second, I believe that when we acknowledge our

power, we are promising ourselves that we intend to live up to who and what we were truly meant to be. That kind of promise carries a great deal of responsibility. We may not feel ready to keep such a promise. Unless we become aware of what owning our personal power means, we will never be able to make clear-sighted choices about how much of it we are willing to claim, loan, or share.

Frankly, although I have learned a lot, I am still not fully at ease with my sense of power. I have learned about different aspects of power as I mature emotionally and spiritually. During this chapter, I will share some of the lessons I've learned about claiming my power in business. Be warned: most of my lessons have been tough. As with all of the stories from my personal experience, I share with the intention of assuring my readers that we all struggle, that we all suffer, during our personal and professional lives. Our suffering is neither unique nor endless. By staying aware, we can emerge from tough times feeling peaceful and serene. I have emerged from these experiences feeling profoundly changed. I have been granted new courage, a deeper knowledge of my identity, and a sense of moving forward on a spiritual level.

Moving Up and Out

A male-dominated corporate culture and a glass ceiling were the eventual undoing of my first corporate experience. As I achieved recognition and awards, I also began to make a lot of money; more money than most of my male superiors at the mid-western corporate headquarters. Several of my upper-level superiors were married to women who had never worked outside their homes. Their life path was very different from mine. Many of these executives started to deliver unfair mandates to me. I had become a *female threat* of sorts and I began to get slaughtered at every turn. Blatant discrimination was an everyday occurrence. I was lied to and pressured to do things I felt were unethical to my customers.

I became concerned about my future and my sanity. My daily life was under constant strain. Surviving at the company was forcing me to choose between doing what I knew to be right and pleasing those in power.

Finally, an incident occurred that I will not recount here. Let it be said that it was so clearly wrong that I knew I could not tolerate the injustice any further. I was still naive enough to believe in morality and honesty as corporate creeds. I had learned that some of my superiors were brutally competitive and vicious, but I was sure the Division President was honest enough to clear up the mess once he knew the whole story.

I decided to take the biggest gamble of my entire career. I would go over everyone's head to the Division President. I had known him for many years and I respected both his apparent sense of fairness and his power. I also knew that this was an enormous risk that could have devastating ramifications on my future with the company. My faith in the Division President's morality combined with how clearly wrong the situation was gave me the courage to take this chance.

I took the risk. The Division President chose not to act on my behalf. I was devastated. I had not begun to comprehend the tremendous strength of the webs of association in a male-dominated company. I hadn't grasped the power of the bonds formed and reinforced by casual conversation in the executive washroom or on the golf course.

They didn't fire me. After all, I was the highest producer in the entire sales force. I knew life would be unbearable under the circumstances. My soul would rot in this male totalitarian environment where I was now marked as a troublemaker. My career with the company was over.

In the mid 1970's another woman had come on board at that same Fortune 500 company and stayed. Judy aspired toward and quickly moved into management. At the time of this incident, Judy was my immediate manager. We shared many of the same qualities and she was definitely driven toward success. She and I became allies and discovered that our backgrounds were much alike. She grew up without a father figure and without corporate role models in her life. She had been convinced that her only way to happiness was to marry well. Both of us were determined to overcome our less fortunate backgrounds through hard work and achievement. Both of us found ourselves being treated unfairly by many of our male managers.

Judy and I commiserated with one another about corporate meetings where the lessons of football or some other male metaphor were preached. Neither of us had a real grasp of the 'boy games' that were the analogies of male corporate management, but we hung onto the belief that achievement and performance could overcome the obviously male culture dominating the corporate structure.

Judy had supported me in doing the right thing in this difficult situation. That led to both of us leaving the company, but measured against the massive male hierarchy, we were just two irritating nits. We left that corporation together about 60 days after the incident. By facing up to the corporate power structure, we watched what had been our *glass ceiling* quickly change into nothing less than a brick wall.

Within hours of our resignations, the Division President flew in from Chicago to convince us of the grave mistake we were making. It was hard to understand why he would be so concerned when it was, in fact, his inaction that had driven us away. His arguments came far too late. We had decided to start our own business.

Learning to Stand Up for Myself

The drama of my experience at the big corporation hadn't been enough to teach me the assertiveness and confidence I needed to really stand up for myself. Judy and I did start a business, but we formed a partnership with a man who had been an executive of the corporation we had just left—giving him majority control of the new venture. I sensed that this move was a mistake, but I lacked the courage to renegotiate the deal. As it turned out, it was a mistake that would haunt us all in the end.

WHEN YOU FAIL TO TAKE RESPONSIBILITY FOR YOUR OWN POWER
YOU WILL NOT ONLY HARM YOURSELF
BUT ALSO THE OTHERS TO WHOM YOU BESTOW FALSE POWER.

We started our new venture in 1982 with soaring spirits, enthusiasm, and optimism. Judy and I had many solid business relationships that were the foundation of our new venture. Success came early. In business only six weeks, we were seeing results as we worked in a sparsely furnished office in a new industrial park just south of San Francisco.

November 1982—I returned to the office from a particularly encouraging day in the field. As I walked into the office, a building maintenance man approached me and asked if either Judy or I was getting a divorce. I thought that was a very odd question. Taken aback, I answered, "No. Why do you ask?"

"You're both being followed by private detectives."

"What? What are you talking about?"

"Yes," he said. "Come upstairs and I'll point them out to you."

Lo and behold, he was right. Two men trying to look inconspicuous in nondescript cars were parked outside. As I left for my next appointment, the man in the yellow and brown sedan followed along behind me.

Judy was outraged when I told her. She immediately called the local police. "Yes," the police chief told her matter-of-factly. "They are definitely following you both. They did register with the police department and they are licensed private detectives. What they are doing is perfectly legal."

Beside herself with rage, Judy said, "Well it may be legal, but if anything happens to either of us it will be on your back! I want them called off immediately."

They were gone that day. We put two and two together and felt quite certain that our former employer was at the bottom of this. We were right. About three days later, our new business venture was served with a Restraining Order that literally shut our doors.

Although we had not broken any laws and there were no grounds for a legal restraining order, big corporations have muscle, money, power, and entire legal departments at their disposal. They were powerful and had influence with judges and lawyers across the state. We went to court the following Monday morning and all charges were dropped when it became clear that it was going to be embarrassing and fruitless for them to pursue. However, the damage was done. Drawing on start-up funding, we spent over $60,000 to defend ourselves in a groundless lawsuit.

Despite our rocky start, business boomed. By the third year we were flying high. Our little venture had grown into the largest company of its kind at the time. We had secured most of the major accounts in California and had offices throughout the state, in Hawaii, and in Illinois. Life was good, but changes were brewing in our technology niche. Things were changing fast. Judy and I were poised and ready to move to new, more advanced technologies. Our male partner was not. He viewed this business as his personal retirement deal, while Judy and I saw it as the genesis of the next high-flying technology innovator.

The fact that we had not demanded equal ownership had returned to haunt us. We parted company. Judy and I stayed together to develop a new leading-edge technology product. We sought out and found some talented programmer/developers. With them, we designed a new, state-of-the-art system for our industry.

Once again (I must be a very slow learner), we naively entered into a business venture without the courage to set up well-defined boundaries and parameters. We wrote a dynamic marketing and business plan but we failed to firm up the corporate ground rules in writing. Our enthusiasm and trusting nature overruled our good sense, and truthfully, we probably hadn't developed the confidence we needed to establish limits, boundaries, and rules. We went forward, trusting that the men we were working with were honorable and trustworthy individuals. Our naiveté came at a very high price this time.

Jointly, we developed an innovative technology system and introduced it to the market. In our shared illusion of the overriding value of achievement and hard work, Judy and I pressed on, stretching to develop market acceptance for this technically advanced system. In our ignorance of the official rules of the game, we were completely unprepared for the onslaught of aggression that would ensue as our business moved into its next phase. After we had laboriously laid all the groundwork, the men involved claimed ownership to the software code for the system and left us high and dry.

I began to cave in on myself emotionally. As much as I had achieved, what was wrong with me? How could I be in such a devastating place all over again? Why couldn't I stand up for myself? And for whatever reason, rather than sticking together, the conflict tore Judy and me apart. Both of us were trying hard to protect our fragile, broken, emotional positions. We refused to speak to each other for over two years.

When we finally came back together, we realized that if we didn't stand up for our rights in this case, there would be no recourse. We decided we had lost too much to keep on losing. We found a wonderful lawyer, a guardian angel for the underdogs of the world. Together, we assembled a case and went after what was rightly ours. We took a stand and were ready to go to the wall for what was right. Waiting so long to assert our rights made our battle exceedingly difficult, but at least we had found the courage to claim what was rightfully ours. Even though the case ended in somewhat of a stalemate, we were vindicated both financially and psychologically.

The lawsuit lasted almost four years and was emotionally excruciating. Judy and I each spent 10-13 days making depositions. Our opponents had hired a slick Brentwood lawyer who tried every trick in the book to dissuade us from seeking legal reparation. As time went on, it was revealed that these two men had climbed over other people's backs besides ours to achieve success. We were not their only victims. Sometimes a person seeking corporate power rationalizes that all is fair on the corporate playing field. The rules for these kinds of players are not about decency, integrity, and honor, but rather a free-for-all with winning as the only goal.

During the lawsuit, I went into a headlong tumble into a seemingly bottomless depression. As my deposition date approached, I felt emotionally incapable of answering questions about the episode. I feared that I would never be able to stand up for myself. I had a complete breakdown. I sat in a therapist's office trying to gather my thoughts and emotions into a position of strength, and instead fell even deeper into despair.

The Corporate Lessons

Corporate games can be rough. Stand up for yourself often and early. Boys begin developing a team consciousness and a certain comfort with aggression from an early age. Team sports teach boys about jockeying for position—about when to plow forward and when to wait. Many more men than women are ready to speak up loud and clear for their ideas and positions. If your ideas deserve merit, if your position needs a push, don't hesitate. Don't spend too much time worrying about who supports your idea. If you know your idea is a solid one, remembering that the truth carries its own power, may give you the incentive to spearhead your idea through your organization to success.

STAND UP FOR YOURSELF OFTEN AND EARLY

Too often in my early career, I stood up for myself too late. A tremendous amount of damage was done by the time I took action on my own behalf. As a result, I could rarely regain the momentum necessary to fuel the idea or regain a strong position.

Hard work and achievement are not enough to succeed. To advance in business, you need to learn the underlying rules of the game and be prepared to play by those rules. Women need to know the rules about sticking together—forming their own team. Often, women who climb the corporate ladder successfully, abandon other women in their political move to place themselves firmly on the male playing field. By the time they reach the desired goal, they are spent. They can hardly keep their positions from sliding, let alone try to help other women up the ladder. It took me 30 years to realize that it was the women on my corporate path that I could count on. Far better than anyone else, they understood what my challenges and struggles were all about. Beyond that, they supported my ideas and, as a team, we were confident enough to take the risk of putting those ideas into the workplace culture.

In the fledging days of my Fortune 500 corporate career I had been "alone" in my office for seven years before Judy was hired and befriended me. I had distanced myself from the secretaries and receptionists because I felt sure that if I was too friendly with them it wouldn't be long before I would be asked to fetch the coffee or type a letter. Before Judy, in the early seventies, a few professional women came and went. A trial-run of trying to compete with 'the boys' and these women tore out the front door for safer harbors. I steered clear of the short-timers to avoid being perceived as a less-than-serious candidate for higher achievement. It was lonely trying to fit in by acting like one of the guys. I believed that if I was to make it to the top, I had to do it on my own.

Fortunately, Judy finally came along. She was a woman with aspirations and a drive that equaled my own. Unlike the others, Judy persevered. We quickly became allies and discovered that we had similar backgrounds. Both of us were determined to overcome our pasts through hard work and achievement. In this one woman friend, I found more than any male mentor ever offered. Judy supported my emotions better, always bolstered my confidence, was there when I needed a friend, understood my feelings, and has remained my friend through a million transitions over my career. I know that her unswerving support has been one of the primary foundations of my success.

Women can't succeed alone. My biggest lesson came when I realized that alone, as a lone-ranger woman, I would never achieve the business success I craved. There are too many basic differences between the sexes. Most women don't really understand what makes up the male psyche—the war games, the sports team analogies, and the ego-driven competitiveness. Even if we did understand, we could not conquer it or adapt our nurturing, consensus-building psyches to be like men's. It seemed that many of the corporate decisions that directly affected my career were made in the men's room where I was not allowed.

Playing it Their Way or Playing a Better Way?

April 1992—My heart pounded like an out-of-control jackhammer, my breath raced. I was standing on a street corner in a strange town and I was afraid. I began to walk. As I rounded the corner, a tidal wave from an unseen ocean washed over me. I was drowning! I awakened drenched in sweat.

My immediate boss at this time appeared to be a typical polished male manager. My hidden need to be accepted and praised blinded me to dangerous personality traits in him that would play against the weakest areas of my emotional makeup and spirit. This new manager, I discovered, believed in *motivation and management by criticism*. He operated like a military general with war on his mind. His strategy was to divide and conquer. I had only been working for this manager three weeks when I received the first major clue that not only was the chemistry between the two of us explosive, it was lethal to my personal vulnerabilities. I was summoned to the manager's office for what he called an early performance review. He sugar-coated his preliminary observations to prepare me for the true reason for the review; serious criticism of my initial short-term performance. He said he felt I had a "couple of problems" and he wanted to point them out to me before I got down the path too far with this company. As it turned out, my "problems" were that I was too enthusiastic and that I tried to do too much. I was devastated. These were my two strongest attributes and were the cornerstone of all of my previous corporate successes.

I had no idea of how deeply this working relationship would dovetail with my insecurities and my inability to stand up for myself. All the understanding and detachment I could muster couldn't relieve me from the constant needling pain that bore into my soul. Another person may have adjusted to this warlike environment easily, but it hammered away at my still-unconscious and very vulnerable inner-self. I began to lose ground quickly.

War games were completely foreign to me. I had no clue about how to deal with this individual. I struggled for almost two years to prove to myself and to those around me that I was up to the challenge of succeeding in spite of constant criticism. I thought that at this point of my career I was aware enough of my strengths and positive characteristics that I could take this manager's inse-cure, nit-picking attitudes lightly. But the stress began to take its toll. How could this have happened to me at this stage of my life? Constant criticism eventually stressed me so much that I would sit at my desk for hours unable to pick up the phone or interact with anyone. I only relaxed when I went on a road trip, returning to my strong roots of performance and personal compas-sion. The military strategy of *divide and conquer,* pitting every person in the office against one another was destroying me and my strong suits of commu-nication, energy, and optimism.

Form a Coup—What a Concept!

Five years later, I was having dinner with a young up-and-coming professional couple. We were discussing business strategies for corporate success, as well as some of the harrowing experiences we'd had. I told about this particularly abu-sive boss and his knack for dividing and separating everyone in the office. He pitted everyone against each other so each individual felt isolated and out of control. He manipulated men and women alike, but the women seemed to fall into his trap more easily. He set up the situation so that we had to defer to him and fight one another to survive on the job. It was a devastating place to work for everyone.

As I explained this to my friends, the young man (a confident young execu-tive) said, "Oh I had a situation like that once. I simply formed a coup."

I was dumbfounded. Never in my wildest imagination would that thought ever have crossed my mind. What is a coup anyway? Another male war game that absolutely would have worked for the people in this *warlord* manager's department. Had we banded together and confronted the manager as a unit, we would have had some power. Wow, what a concept! I was blown away by the straightforward, simple strategy this young man would use to deal with a person like my *warlord* manager.

For most of my career, I never saw nor accepted the big and small truths about the difference in boys and girls (men and women). I didn't have a clue about football, baseball, or for that matter, about any of the team sports. I had even less understanding about waging war and forming coups than I did about team sports. Being a war-general, a team player, or a team leader was beyond my comprehension.

How can a woman learn to play corporate War Games? How can she win in a business setting where corporate strategies are based on football, automobile racing, and aggressive team sports? Perhaps women cannot win if the rules remain in the male domain. When a woman understands the rules and comes to understand that these games are the driving force in many corporate arenas, she can change the rules. She must be smart enough to know that if she cannot win with a frontal assault, she must use her innate talents to develop a methodology to work with the truth. A strategy then can be designed to work with the war/team mentality while not abandoning spiritual principles.

Never having played war games and never having been a male, I'm not sure of all the answers to these male-oriented corporate culture issues but I do know that I must have the courage to be true to myself. The business career I chose is my passion and my life's purpose. I have a right and a responsibility to proceed with dignity.

Why Buck the System?

We are, in small but insidious ways, corporate codependents. Corporations are only too happy to let us believe that they hold our power and that we would be happier, better off really, if we contributed our bit of personal power to their system by following their rules and subscribing to their beliefs about profit and success.

Like little children, if we surrender our power to these systems, they will take care of us. They will decide what's best. They will use our resources, our energy, to feed the corporate giant. It's especially easy to fall into the trap of being a good 'team player' when we're young and are still forming our own personal identities. The structure, the rules, and the material benefits may feel more valid because they are clearly and visibly established. When we follow pre-ordained rules, we don't take responsibility for formulating and living by our own principles. The problem for many of us comes after we've lived by the corporate rulebook for a time and we find ourselves feeling increasingly uncomfortable as we continue to follow rules that experience has shown us make little sense and go against our internal beliefs.

The corporate system demands our energy, but only within certain parameters. If we put out too much energy, if we shine too brightly, we unbalance and short-circuit the system. Making too much money, coming up with too radical an idea or progressing too fast, sets red flags flying in corporations. By the same token, underachieving sucks energy from the system. If we work for firms with 60-hour-a-week expectations, we may threaten the system by taking weekends or holidays off.

I lacked business skills and experience as I moved into the corporate environment. Without social expertise or spiritual strength to support me, I did my best to follow the rules of the established power system. It took me quite some time to realize that the corporation was not where my power truly came from or where it belonged. It took more time for me to learn where my power ended and where the company's began.

Your boss is not your power. The CEO is not your power. Don't give pieces of yourself to those who would claim your power for material gain alone. Wherever you are in the corporate structure, you still have the power in your own life. You can choose how you think and act. You can have a sense of dignity and esteem in whom you are and what you have to contribute to the people around you. Corporations often bestow power upon individuals at certain levels, but in *the world of the soul,* this is all nonsense. We are all just human beings trudging along, or dancing along the corporate road to a life of peace and love.

If you are unhappy in your corporate position, take the time to analyze your situation. Maybe you are on the wrong road. As I got my own values in order, I understood the equality of peers and 'superiors' alike. I was convinced that all people are equally fragile and vulnerable after the high level executive in my first corporate job shot himself. I was reminded once again recently, when the highest-ranking US Naval officer committed suicide. No one is immune to daily struggles and occasional despair.

Without a cognizant connection to the soul, humans are doomed to isolation and despair. Rich and tangible soul values are perhaps more important today than they have ever been. We face an all-consuming, mighty corporate tidal wave. This force is fed by materialistic consumption, cutthroat competition, and financial profit.

To survive and grow as whole human beings, we must each dig deep into our soul-centers to search for the powerful eternal values and put these values to work in our corporate lives—in the boardrooms and in the mailrooms.

Some Simple Spiritual Rules for the Corporate Road

- Get your own house in order as best you can. This is a lifetime job for all of us, but we can't let up on this task. As we develop our core spiritual nature our internal confidence increases.

- What we are not aware of dominates everything we do. Awareness doesn't mean our issues disappear (sorry), but we can only manage those issues we're aware of.

- Make peace with where you came from. You cannot change it.

The Power of Inventories

Learn to take honest inventories of your strengths and weaknesses. Write them down on paper. When seen on paper, the mystery disappears. Write down:

What you do well	What you like doing	What you feel comfortable doing	What you'd like to accomplish in your lifetime

Writing allows you to make the journey from your head to your heart. In your heart, your dreams can come to fruition and you will discover your true calling on this human adventure. Taking a written inventory is a tool to help you create boundaries and priorities. Boundaries keep you focused on your own areas of influence and priorities help you stay focused on where you want to go in your corporate career.

When doing honest inventories of your strengths, weaknesses, and weirdnesses, you will find peace and happiness. Rigorous self-honesty opens the doorway to a rewarding corporate life and a peaceful life for your soul.

Risk Taking:

- Stand up for yourself and your ideas early and often. Risk-taking is a perfected skill of the super corporate achiever.

- Your life is not a mistake. Everything about you is valuable. Even your negative side is a teaching tool that provides character growth, inner strength, and soul development. Successful people on this earthbound adventure have learned to put their ideas into action in order to achieve success. When their ideas are wrong, they learn the lessons at hand and move on.

- Those of us who sit on the sidelines in fear, miss out on the full life experience. Take a chance. Use your mistakes as lessons and opportunities for growth.

Sometimes taking a chance requires courage and consultation. Some time back I was invited to join a group of the most successful and well-known consultants in my niche of the technology business. My first inclination was to join immediately. Paradoxically, relying on others for identity and support has often resulted in having to play the caregiver. So this time I consulted some close friends before joining. They helped me see that there was little to gain and much to lose by taking this step. In the past, this counsel wouldn't have deterred me from hitching my wagon to someone else's star. I informed the group that I wouldn't be joining. Acknowledging my own self-sufficiency left me with a real sense of confidence and well-being. I was able to take the chance. I wanted to find out what I could do on my own with this earthbound excursion.

Anger

If anger is an issue, and it is with most of us, become cognizant of the issues that still block you from a peaceful existence. Look at The Anger Spreadsheet in Chapter 7 and determine how many monster madnesses you've buried deep inside. Bring them out. Get angry. Look at the injustices you've suffered. Be honest. Feel the pain and place the blame. If your anger is significant, (often it is), line up a therapist. Work it through. Beat the pillows, pound the punching bag—do whatever it takes. True forgiveness only comes when anger is exposed to fresh air and light. When you forgive old transgressions, you reclaim the energy (and the power) you've been committing to them since they happened. Forgiveness is the road to a peaceful heart.

Health

This is a time also to look at the beneficial steps you need to take for the betterment of your body. It seems we were only given one vehicle for this earthbound adventure. To make the most of this lifetime, it behooves us to learn about the care and maintenance of our physical bodies.

Do what you can today. Set up some habits that you can live with and practice everyday. Feel good about what you can do, knowing that as you grow, you will do more.

Illusions of Power—Lessons in the Street

Let go of your burdens and your treasures.

Several years ago as I was driving through San Francisco, I spotted a homeless man trying to cross the street. The man had three shopping carts loaded with everything imaginable. There were pieces of cardboard, scraps of newspaper, old cans and bottles, filthy ragged clothes, old shoes, and a scruffy black and white cat. The carts literally overflowed. If the man moved too swiftly, the carts teetered and his treasured possessions toppled. Each cart was tied with an old rope to the next, so that as he pulled the first along, the others followed. As he struggled across the street, some of his treasures spilled from the carts. The man stooped, picked them up, and returned them to their piles. He continued slowly on his way, pushing the cart with the cat as a passenger and pulling the other two precariously up onto the sidewalk.

He had a furtive look in his eyes as he protected his possessions. Clearly, these possessions were all he owned. He looked like he was king of the street people, the CEO of his Corporate Cart World when it came to having the most stuff. Yet, what a burden his 'treasures' brought him. He couldn't take his eyes off them for fear someone would try to steal them. Something as simple as crossing the street was an enormous task. Surely his possessions and treasures narrowed his world to a few square blocks. His position, possessions, and treasures were his prison.

Was I like this man? Yes, I'm afraid so. We all cling to our worldly goods. As they do for the man in the street, these worldly goods create prisons for us. Let go of your pet ideas, your little identities, your rigid belief systems, and your treasure trove of possessions. We are on a great adventure of the soul. The corporate world is merely one pathway for this adventure. It presents us with opportunities to grow our souls and live out our dramas. It is a game, not an all-consuming quest. The true quest is our soul's path. We must not let ourselves be burdened by rigid ideas and false identities.

Illusions of Powerlessness—Not Formally Educated

My mother used to always say, "Don't let your education rob you of the brains you were born with." Attitude and desire outweigh education and degrees.

Choice, not chance, determines our destiny. It is not formal education, culture, upbringing, gender, race, or any outer force that keeps us from happiness and success in the corporate world or in life. It is the choices we make both consciously and unconsciously.

Education, as it turns out, is a matter of experience. Every experience teaches us lessons for living. Whether the experiences come from joy or pain, the lessons teach us about life, our soul, and our purpose. The lessons enlighten us to our true human nature. All of us are called upon to participate in the life we have been given and to learn the best we can from daily experiences. Our responses to the life and lessons we are given help us each to identify our purpose and become acquainted with our personal soul-selves.

Paying attention to how you act and react will help you access clues to your inner nature. As your understanding deepens, you can take charge of some of your reactions. Every circumstance you encounter can become your pathway to higher spiritual education.

Value Your Lessons *(tell your story and write your own book)*

Recognize the value in your own lessons, rather than only embracing the lessons of gurus or even good mentors. Your own story and lessons are fascinating, powerful, and meaningful, not only to you, but to many others who cross your path. Life is not just some random path on which we are hopelessly and blindly stumbling along. It is a blessed path toward fulfillment of our purpose. Each of us has a life-path full of spiritual lessons, but if we are insecure and afraid, as I was for most of my early years, then it is easier to share and live by the lessons of others. But this is not who we are or why we are here. Each human spirit is a unique miracle. Each of us has special gifts to deliver. We do not need mentors or gurus. Our internal spirits have the answers we seek.

For me, the reward of reaching my 40's was that I had begun to understand that my lessons have impact on others and my lessons can be shared to help others. My lessons turn out to be the soul-food that those who cross my path hunger for. If this is true for me, it is true also for you. Your lessons are the essence of your human experience and they are the magical thread that joins your soul to others.

Trust who you are. You are not a mistake, you are a miracle. You are perfect, created to bring a unique and wonderful presence to those around you, a presence no one else can bring. Cherish it.

How can you find and own your own power?

- Take a risk.

- Identify and nurture your soul ideas.

- Don't personalize or internalize failure.
- Trust in your divine destiny.

6

Principle Four—Perseverance: Hanging On in the Dark Times

A Story of Perseverance—amidst the chaos of a grim and bloody battle, a soldier suddenly dropped his rifle. He wandered and then stooped to pick up a scrap of paper. He looked at it briefly and then let it flutter to the ground. He wandered off again, finding more scraps of paper, picking them up, and letting them fall back to the ground.

Concerned about this strange behavior, his superior officer had the man taken to the hospital. Once there, the mute soldier continued to pick up scraps of paper, always looking at them carefully, and always dropping them again. He was checked into a psychiatric hospital, where his strange behavior continued.

After months of this consistently bizarre behavior, it was decided to discharge the soldier from the Army. His superior officer delivered the discharge papers personally and upon handing the notice to him, the soldier examined the notice, as he had examined all the slips of paper he'd picked up over the past months and he exclaimed, "This is it! This is what I was looking for!"

In this story, told by the late mystic Anthony de Mello[1], we see that even though our behavior may seem odd to others, our persistent belief and consistent actions can indeed create miraculous outcomes.

If I had not persevered on the personal, professional, and spiritual fronts, I shudder to think what my life would be like now—*if I were still alive*. In fact, I

---

1. Fr. Anthony de Mello, 1931–1987

may well be living this life to learn lessons in perseverance. I see my life as a metaphor for one of those crazy survival excursions that so many people join in the midst of personal or career crises. Survival programs like Outward Bound (or in my case, running the New York City Marathon) are experiences that make you dig deep to discover what your mind, body, and soul can survive. They often make us see that the human experience alone is far more rewarding than a healthy corporate balance sheet, an illustrious new IPO (*Initial Public Offering*), or a handful of stock options.

Maybe our experience here on earth really is a *Soul Survival excursion*. Perhaps we all signed on for this adventure on some other physical plane. I could imagine myself sitting around drinking lattes with my soul mates. One of them may have turned to me and said, "I've been training for a while. I'm in good shape. I think I'll sign up to do that Earth Endurance Program. Let's do it together, Lynne. You've been training too. You're in good shape. You can do it."

I considered. "I'm ready for a new challenge. Yes, I'll do the *corporate course* this time. I hear it's a tough course for women right now, a real character builder. I'll bet I can make it to the end."

Perhaps we chose to do this earthbound adventure with many others who would love us throughout our daily journey through the experience of being human. Maybe the people we know now to be our soul mates, our families, our corporate associates, and even our adversaries, were around that table with us, deciding how the adventure would play out. However it was all arranged, I feel sure that we came here to grow our souls and develop our character.

My ability to persevere has moved me forward by leaps and bounds in my career and my personal life. Spiritual perseverance is different from tangible realities because it involves letting go of control and 'going with the flow', but it is the same in that it is an unswerving commitment that yields dramatic results over time.

IF YOU HAVE MADE MISTAKES...THERE IS ALWAYS ANOTHER CHANCE FOR YOU...YOU MAY HAVE A FRESH START ANY MOMENT YOU CHOOSE,

FOR THIS THING WE CALL 'FAILURE' IS NOT THE FALLING DOWN,
BUT THE STAYING DOWN.
Mary Pickford, a silent screen star, 1892–1979

Don't Let Failures Keep you From Succeeding!

March 1978—My career was on the rise at the Fortune 500 Company. Our national sales meeting was in Boulder, Colorado that year. I had been with the corporation for about eight years. I had received several awards and this year, I was being recognized as the top corporate achiever in my region.

My immediate manager and his regional manager were proud of me. They were fond of bragging about having the first up-and-coming woman in the corporation on their team. I was pleased about the attention and excited about my success.

At this national meeting, we were introducing a new product as part of the systems we would be selling in the upcoming year. Our agenda at the meeting included introducing the product and then doing small-group practice demonstrations to our peers. Although I had confidence in making presentations to clients by now, I remained completely awed by my business associates. I was very nervous about doing this demonstration to a group of my peers. When my turn came, everyone expected me, the regional top achiever, to breeze right through my presentation. In fact, both my boss and his boss expected me to set a shining and professional example for the newer people in the company.

I was a miserable failure. I sweated profusely. My heart pounded and I choked on every word. I wasn't the only one who thought I'd done a poor job. My performance was ranked at the bottom of everyone else's—newcomers included. It was a real embarrassment for my bosses and me.

The Corporate Soul Survival Lesson

The year following the Colorado meeting, I went on to sell more hardware and systems than anyone else in the entire company. By a very large margin, I outsold every other salesperson on the very product that I had been unable to demonstrate to my peers in Colorado. During the same year, I became the first woman with the company ever to be named National Salesperson of the Year. Two years later, I was the first woman member of the prestigious Presidents' Club. I had risen from the ashes of self-destruction to become a respected achiever and a corporate super star. Sometimes hard work and perseverance seemed to be the only qualifications in my tool-bag, but they were enough for this achievement. The lesson here? Don't let failure get you down. Keep on trying, keep on facing your fears and let your skills shine through. Hard work and perseverance will see anyone up the ladder. Motivational speakers and trainers alike always fall back on these tools as the bedrock of success.

It is hard to quantify or teach perseverance. But it can be learned. It is learned through seeing events in our lives as lessons and committing ourselves to learning from them. These lessons will give us the faith we need to move forward time and time again, despite all negative appearances.

It would be no exaggeration to claim that at least 35 to 45 percent of all of the deals I ever closed were someone else's deals. They were 'dead deals', deals that the other salespeople had given up on long ago. Not me. I believed in myself at that level. I truly believed in the quality of the product, service, and commitment that each customer would receive from me. I would not walk out the door until I'd had the chance to demonstrate that commitment to the client. I did not give up.

All of the so-called mistakes I've made have been the fodder for spiritual lessons that are today shaping my inner peace, humility, and happiness. These spiritual lessons are the ones that have brought me to a place where I am doing something that I love doing with my career. I could not have gotten here without my 'many mistakes'.

Courage is in the Doing

Corporate courage is a byproduct of *doing*. Corporate coincidences are miracles that we recognize only when we are ready to respond to them.

I have never considered myself a person of courage. Actually, I've thought just the opposite of myself. For as long as I can remember, I have been burdened by an endless litany of fears: fear of flying, fear of roller coasters, fear of failure, fear of rejection, fear of countless bogeymen. Making the choice to persevere has shown me that even I can develop courage.

The Fear of Flying

Like many of my generation, I grew up before air travel was commonplace. My first flight was at the age of eleven. It was under very stressful circumstances brought about by a family emergency. My dear and drunk father had gone to prison and my distraught mother was taking us back to her family home in Utah. I was being uprooted from everything I had known in my life. This was not in any way an adventure or pleasant experience. Added to the despair of my family's crisis was my mother's fear of air travel and her terror about her uncertain life circumstances. I remember little of that first flight, other than along with my brother and sister, I got a pair of flight wings pinned on my collar.

This was a journey leading away from everything I knew as good and safe in life. It led me into a strange world for which I was ill-prepared. I left a small, rural California country town and a school where the most social thing we did was square dancing on the blacktop playground and entered a big city school with teenagers who were far more socially mature than anyone I had ever known. They danced with each other and the girls seemed to have more than a passing interest in the boys. I didn't get it. I felt awkward and socially retarded; a Martian dropped off by mistake in a foreign world.

Airline flight, for me, began as a symbol of leaving safety and security for unknown territory. As a young adult, my flight experience was reserved for emergency situations. My father died. My aunt died. Until I entered business, everything about flying was a fearful and dramatic emergency.

Once I became a corporate citizen, flying was required for regional events and conferences. Early on, I fortified myself for every flight with alcohol or tranquilizers. This strategy seemed to work well. I just got loaded and strapped on the seat belt. At least I showed up where I was supposed to be (often a little worse-for-wear and hung-over).

After my first *abyss experience* I had stopped drinking and I no longer could mask my feelings with chemicals. That bridge to safety (or at least numbness) was burned behind me. Flying became torturous. I was furious. Without chemical numbing, I was trapped in fear. I was thoroughly excited about creating a new corporate career for myself and I wanted to move ahead with my work life, but I could only do it moving about freely in the corporate world. Flying was a big part of the career adventure stretching out before me.

What could I do? With each passing year, flying became more terrifying. Then the unthinkable happened. I was on a flight bound for Hawaii when the plane lost an engine. They tried to reassure me and all of the other passengers that this was really nothing, but their efforts were futile. I was frozen with fear. The plane returned to San Francisco Airport. They repaired the engine and somehow I forced myself back aboard and went on to Hawaii. I guess the spirit of perseverance was the only thing that got me through that. I kissed the ground on Maui and wondered how I would ever get home.

When we returned I was deeply shaken. My fear had become an out-of-control monster. It threatened to build a fortress around my freedom and put an end to my otherwise rewarding work life. Air travel was sure to be a requirement for advancement. Pain and perseverance forced me to seek an answer.

I called the local airport and tracked down a *Fear of Flying*[2] clinic. It cost a lot of money, but I had to do it. Once a week I attended a behavior modification and reeducation program. The course transformed both my fear and my thought processes. By week seven, I was reeducated. My spirit was singing again. Week eight was to be an actual flight from San Francisco to Oakland and San Jose. But my week eight was going to be a completely different trial-flight experience.

Three months earlier I had left the Fortune 500 Corporation and started a new business with two of my peers. It was a risky step on an entrepreneurial adventure. Due to our long-term relationships, many of our previous accounts were eager to stay with us and even help in our new venture. Our former employer had not been happy about the situation. With deep pockets and strong political and judicial ties in Chicago, they had hired private detectives to follow us and eventually had closed the doors to our business with a Restraining Order. This had happened during the seventh week of my *Fear of Flying* clinic. My trial-flight was a red-eye to Chicago. I would be appearing in court on Monday morning to get the judge to reopen the doors to my business. This airplane trip turned out to be a positive journey with a successful outcome.

We won all of the concessions we needed to move on to develop our new corporation and within three years, that corporation became a powerhouse in our industry. We gained worldwide attention with our skyrocketing success. After a rocky start, for the first time in my life, flying became attached to a

---

2.   Fear Of Flying Clinics—www.fofc.com

powerful and positive experience. My fear of flying lesson was clearly multifaceted.

The *fear* turned out to be made up of a lot of other little fears. I learned that I was more afraid when I was on an out-bound flight than when I was returning home. This wasn't a fear of flying; this was a fear of leaving all that was familiar. I also noticed, after sitting one night in the cockpit of a Boeing 737, that I would feel just fine if I could be at the controls. The fear was not of flying itself, but of giving control of my life to someone I didn't even know.

The Corporate Soul Survival Lesson

My fear of flying was an illusion. Airplane flying is the safest of all forms of travel, far safer than the car I jump into without a second thought. When I finally learned that my chances of dying in an airplane were less than my chances of winning the lottery, I began forming a more realistic view of flying. Win the lottery? I don't think so. The biggest thing I ever won was a bingo game.

Corporate courage is the byproduct of perseverance and *doing*. By facing these fears, by doing what I've needed to do to calm them, I've learned new lessons about living a spiritual life in a corporate world. Many of my business associates suffer fears similar to mine. Most are afraid to voice them and they choose not to do anything about them. As I discovered in my fear of flying classes, my fears were not the fears I thought they were. Only after I began to understand them was I able to manage them. It is the feelings we have and don't understand that manage us. Once we come to understand them, then we can manage our feelings. My world would have gotten smaller and smaller if I had not persevered and faced these fears by seeking the help I needed. I knew other people weren't afraid of flying, so why not learn from them? They surely knew something I didn't. As I've persevered and faced my fears, I've learned that they are merely bogeymen with only as much power as I grant them. Facing fears, walking through them, reveals the illusions as they truly are.

As I move through the corporate world today, I see pain, stress, and destruction everywhere, because most of us are afraid to admit that we are afraid. Fear is not acknowledged or respected in the minds of the corporate majority. Acknowledging our fears reveals our vulnerability, which is usually off-limits in business relationships. Yet, fear manages us in powerful ways. It takes a toll in physical well-being and tears apart sweet relationships. For me, life has been much easier since I can just say; *This makes me feel afraid.*

As we learn to be more honest with our feelings, we give others permission to be honest with their feelings. Will the aura of invulnerable corporate power come crashing down as a result of this new honesty? Of course not. In fact, I believe a stronger corporate foundation will arise from the power of spiritually alive human beings expressing normal human feelings.

Perseverance Power Again

January 1994—Shortly after pulling myself out of my second *abyss experience*, an East Coast company called and asked if I would come and speak at their national corporate meeting. I was thrilled. Of course I would. "Where is the meeting," I asked.

"Lake Placid, New York."

"Sure, I can come." *Where is Lake Placid, I wondered.* "When do you need me?"

"Mid-January."

I wondered what the weather was like in Lake Placid. How could I say no? I was starting a new business. They wanted to hire me and I would go. We made the arrangements. They sent a deposit check and the day came. Until this trip, I had done a fair amount of corporate traveling, but it had always been well-defined. Either I knew the area, I was with a group, or it was in a major metropolitan area where I could flag a taxi or figure out straightforward logistics for the trip.

As I made my reservations, I realized that I couldn't get to Albany, New York (the closest airport) before evening. Just getting to New York would be an all-day trip from California. Night driving in a strange place is not easy for me. In truth, I probably could be considered night-blind.

While pondering my upcoming trip, I asked a friend from the East Coast how far the drive from Albany to Lake Placid was. Friends in California were reassuring. Only a couple of hours on the freeway. That sounded easy enough. Since I'm from California, I hadn't driven in snow country much. Oh well, I reasoned, *suit up and show up.*

The biggest snowstorm of the season barreled down on the East Coast the weekend before my scheduled trip. *I thought surely they'd cancel, but no—no cancellation.* I got on the plane Monday morning to arrive for a 7:00 A.M. session Tuesday morning. It was almost 5:00 P.M. on Monday when I finally arrived in Albany. I went directly to the rental car counter.

"I'm going to Lake Placid," I explained. "My friends tell me it's about two hours on the freeway. Do you have a map?"

"Two hours? Who told you that? It's about two and a half hours on the freeway then another hour over the mountain."

Oh my God! "Well, do you have one of those all-terrain trucks?"

"One just came in, but I can't give it to you. It has no gas and needs to be washed."

"Forget the wash and I'll put gas in myself. Just help me load my baggage and I'll be on my way. I've got to get there tonight." I was off.

I'd been true to my motto *real women don't pump gas* for about five years. Nothing upsets me more than standing by the gas pump in an expensive designer suit and having gasoline dripping all over me. But in Albany, it looked like I'd have little choice. I needed to get going, so I pulled into the first gas station I spotted. I'd had little opportunity to practice my ice-walking, so as soon as I got out of the truck (*all-terrain vehicle*) I immediately slipped on the ice. The temperature was about ten (10°F) degrees above zero at 6:00 P.M. Of course, I had no gloves or hat. My fingers froze to that blasted gasoline nozzle as I tried to fill the tank on my truck and my ears turned downright brittle with cold. Who know these things in California?

I got the gas and was on my way. Once I was on the freeway, it didn't seem too bad. *Just like home*, I reassured myself. It's just a freeway with everyone going home from work. *I can handle this.* I drove for awhile. Soon it was dark and there was less traffic. I felt like I might be climbing at this point, maybe into the mountains. The thermometer reading the outside temperature was dropping. Now it was −5°F degrees. My God, I realized if this truck (*all-terrain vehicle*) stalls, I'll freeze to death. There were almost no cars now. Occasionally a big semi-truck passed, showering ice and rocks all over my windshield. I pressed on.

I hadn't seen a freeway sign for a long time. *Where was I?* Finally a freeway sign, big, green, and familiar: Montreal–190 miles. *Oh my God, Montreal! Where am I going?* The temperature drops to −7°F degrees. I was alone.

Finally, I couldn't take the strain anymore. I had to stop and rest. Eventually I saw a turn-off; a hopeful indication. There was a roadside sign with a picture of a little bed, a gas pump, and a knife and fork! I was sure it meant motel, gas, and food. I pulled off to find a place to stay. *I'd get to Lake Placid in the morning*, I thought as I drove off at the exit. It looked pretty deserted at first, but then I caught sight of a small light. It looked like a gas station. It was. I pulled up and got out. The station had one little pump. Inside the glass office sat two men who bore an uncanny resemblance to the villains in the movie, *Deliverance*[3].

Please God, watch out for me! I went inside. "Excuse me, where are the motels and restaurants?"

"No motel or restaurant here, lady."

"So," I asked, "where is the closest place to stay over night?"

"Lake Placid," they reply.

"Where is Lake Placid?" My tone of voice must have sunk to pleading by now. I was exhausted and afraid.

"Up the road to the next exit, 20 miles or so, then get off the freeway and drive over the hill," the villains advised.

With no alternative, I climbed back in my truck. The temperature was now a frigid –9°F degrees. *What kind of woman am I, I mused? My husband is sitting at home in California by a nice cozy fire…Why am I out here in this god-forsaken place all by myself? Please God, keep this truck running.*

I continued on the freeway and got off at the next exit. A very small sign pointed toward Lake Placid. Now I was on a narrow two-lane road covered with ice and snow. I expected to be even more afraid but strangely, I said a little prayer for help and I felt very calm.

The beautiful snow on the surrounding countryside instilled an indescribable sense of peace. I started over the mountain at a serene speed, feeling strangely safe, protected, and quiet in this white wonderland so far from my California home. Most of the next hour was a beautiful drive. No other cars were out but occasionally soft yellow lights shined forth from cozy little mountain homes as I drove on. It was very cold (–13°F degrees).

I pushed on. Discouragement and bone-deep exhaustion set in. I wondered if I'd ever see civilization again. It had been more than four hours since I landed at the airport in Albany. What was I doing out here? *I quit!* But how could I quit? There was no one to quit to. I was there. There was no going back now.

Fatigue blurred my vision. When would I see some sign of civilization? Driving over the next hill, I saw a red light high in the sky. What was it? I knew the Olympics had been at Lake Placid once. Yes, that's what it was. It was the ski jump, high in the sky with a red light atop. I'd made it! I cruised

---

3.   *Deliverance*, Warner Bros., 1972

gratefully into the sleepy little village, got out, and asked directions. I found the hotel, ordered a hamburger, and dropped into grateful sleep.

My session began the next morning at 7:00 A.M.. I had never even met these people, but I showed up and there they were. Introductions and then I was on until 6:00 P.M. that night. The training went well. The information I shared was appreciated and in the end I felt gratified. They all trundled off to a company awards dinner, leaving me alone to worry about driving back to the airport in the morning. At least, now, I knew it would take about four hours and I had a plane to catch at 11:00 A.M.

By 6:00 A.M. the next morning, it was snowing. *What next?* I asked the desk clerk if he could show me how to use my rental truck's 4-wheel drive feature. They thought I was a riot. *(She doesn't know how to drive a 4-wheel drive. Ha ha!)* Things didn't seem so funny to me.

I climbed back aboard the truck and headed back to Albany. I made it in time to catch my little prop plane to cart me, bouncing all of the way, down to Newark, New Jersey, where I had an appointment with an international company that had asked me to write their training program. I thought the adventure was over when I left Lake Placid until I tried to get out of the Newark Airport and then get on to the New Jersey Turnpike. Give me Lake Placid! The entire trip was a challenge. This adventure was much like completing my first marathon. Afterward, I felt like I could do anything. Call me. Ask me to go anywhere. I can do it. My fears are gone. I can do it.

Corporate courage—all courage, for that matter—comes from doing. The biggest gifts always come from the hardest challenges. Just remembering that bit of wisdom is a worthwhile goal.

A Word About Miracles and Perseverance

Miracles are always in the making, but if we don't hang in there we won't get the chance to set the miracles in motion and we certainly won't be there to witness the outcome. Coincidences are just miracles that appear when we are open and ready to respond to them. They occur when we finally surrender to present circumstances, when we can stop frantically flailing and look around at the advantages of being *where we are* rather than in the circumstances we had imagined for ourselves.

I've heard countless members of Alcoholics Anonymous say if they had written down all the goals they had for their lives during their first thirty days of sobriety in AA, they would have woefully shortchanged themselves. They didn't have an inkling of the joys and opportunities that lay ahead. Setting rigid goals at that point would only have limited their achievements. The truth is that we don't know what will make our hearts sing until we encounter it. Focusing on extremely precise and rigid goals can prevent us from recognizing delightfully unexpected opportunities.

This is not to say goals are unimportant. I do use goals in my personal and professional life. I just don't worry too much if they don't materialize precisely on schedule or in the exact form that I had visualized. I don't suffer much disappointment when an achievement isn't exactly what I expected it to be. Divine destiny often has a much greater plan to deliver.

I need only to trust in divine destiny and to continue to stay present for myself every day. My overall goal is to have enough courage to walk into the day trusting that things will fall into place just as they're meant to be.

The Power of Persistence

Nothing can take the place of persistence.
Talent will not;
Nothing is more common than unsuccessful men with talent.
Genius will not;
Unrewarded genius is almost a proverb.
Education will not;
The world is full of educated derelicts.
Persistence and determination alone are omnipotent.
The slogan "Press On" has solved, and always will solve, the problems of the human race.
Calvin Coolidge—*Thirtieth President of the United States*, 1872–1933

7

Responsibility and Authenticity

Healing Anger

Much of the corporate world is a bubbling hot pot of anger. Just under the lid lies a poisonous brew of red-hot madness ready to boil over. Have you ever been around a rage-aholic? They might only blow once in a great while, but the energy is always present, keeping them and us constantly on edge. Rage-aholics use their energy as a control device. If children are raised with raging parents, they become *eggshell walkers*, always treading lightly for fear of the mighty explosion. Corporate life is charged with this powerful negative energy.

Many of us suffer from anger that was initially fueled by being raised in an environment of conditional love and emotional neglect. We missed the consistent nurturing and unconditional love we needed to feel fully accepted and worthwhile for who we really are, rather than for what we achieve. Most of us were loved for our achievements and were rewarded when we got good grades or performed well in sports. Resentments grew the more we felt we had to hide our true selves and show only our 'worthy' selves. We grew up in an achievement-based society. The corporate environment presents us with a familiar emotional dynamic that makes it very easy to transfer our anger from home to workplace. If you aren't achieving at work, you are perceived as worthless and unwanted. Even though material achievement has nothing to do with our true self-worth, because it fits our social conditioning so closely, it certainly feels like it does.

Many physically mature men and women remain hampered by hidden anger from their childhoods. Children are completely dependent upon their parents. They are unable to see and accept the damage that is done to them as human beings while they grow up. They have no comparative models. The common reasoning about damage done to them during their childhood is, "My parents did the best they could." This is often true, but in many cases they did a lousy job.

To heal my anger, I needed to see the truth about its source. I needed to transfer the blame from me to the appropriate individuals (in some cases, my parents). Of course, this is a double-edged sword. I am a parent. My children were also victims of my unconscious child-rearing ideas, my selfishness and neglect. As adults, it is time for us to look closely at the damage done to us, as well as the damage we've done to others. We don't do this to enter into a scene of hatred or remorse. We do it to make peace with the truth. Looking at the source of our anger is frequently a painful grieving experience that involves letting go of our childish ideas and ideals.

I use the three-column spreadsheet below to view anger. I've been in all three columns. The hardest thing for me to do was place blame and feel my anger, but I know from experience that without feeling the anger and placing the blame, forgiveness is meaningless.

The healing column is a three-step process. The identifying and blaming (possibly confronting) is the formula for healing and wholeness.

The Anger Spreadsheet

If I feel:	If I feel:	If I want:
Anger at Another Keeps me fixated on the other person	**Anger at Myself** Blame self or forgive before I've fully identified the wrong-doing	**Healing Approach** Identify, name and see the wrong-doing
Keeps me a victim	Brings depression	Fosters forgiveness
Can lead to homicide	Can lead to suicide	Heals wounds

Like all of life's challenges, anger is something only you can change in yourself. Get honest with yourself; try to uncover feelings that may have been locked down long ago. You may think this exposure of your vulnerable self will make you weak, but it won't. You will never have true strength, character, and power until you first identify, accept, and conquer your anger.

Remember this: the angry and egotistical men or women you encounter on your corporate journey are the ones who are most afraid. *These are fragile and brittle people.* Their fears may be very deep-rooted and may be a life-long burden.

A final observation about anger: Many of us can't admit it when we are wrong. We handle our obvious blunders by not talking about them and moving on. Life is far easier when we can admit and accept our fallibility. Take a chance and learn to be wrong once in awhile. Learn to say, "I don't know" or "I was wrong." Life is much more rewarding when we can admit our fragility, flaws, and humanness. When we're *perfect*, we can never change our minds, admit our mistakes, or be downright frivolous. We become frozen in fear. When things go wrong for us, we find ourselves clinging to the precipice, hanging on, and staring into the abyss.

Let go. *It's going to be all right.*

Fear and Anger

Fear is at the root of most corporate dysfunction. Anger develops out of such fear. Anger is the surface emotion that is perceived as strong and powerful, but when we scratch the surface of our anger, up surges fear.

The corporate world has created an image of the polished and fearless businessperson who cannot be afraid. Showing fear is interpreted as weakness. We can go days and weeks without hearing a single co-worker say, "I'm scared. This is a scary situation."

This is an unnatural restriction of feelings for the human soul. We all have fears. We fear death, sickness, competition, the opinions of others, our performance failures, flying, poverty, commitment, and on and on. Our corporate habitats will become healthy when we find the freedom to express our human feelings without concerns of reprisal. It takes a courageous leader to step forward and openly express vulnerable feelings.

Today I'm surrounded with incredibly honest people. I've learned to openly express many personal and professional experiences that I once was afraid to discuss. I need to honestly express my feelings and share my experiences to have inner peace. Once I started being honest and fully expressing myself, my colleagues felt safe doing the same. I found that many people had experiences similar to mine. Sharing those unpopular feelings of fear and failure or embarrassment actually brought me stronger connections with my co-workers. So many of us share the same feelings and experiences, but because we are afraid to openly express them, we may feel trapped in the corporate camouflage of a relentlessly upbeat achievement orientation that keeps us feeling isolated and dishonest.

The Abyss

Throughout time, people have set out on quests to find themselves, journeys to discover personal meaning, and peace in their lives. Often such journeys begin with a crisis. This isn't surprising. When we're happy and comfortable, we want things to remain the same. When we are unsettled, sick, and in despair, we seek change. In desperation, we seek answers both to greater mysteries and basic problems. And although we may seek and find help as we struggle, the important lessons we learn are developed at an inner-soul level and on our own.

I grew up in the California countryside and farmland of the 40's and 50's. As a small child, my parents issued severe warnings about the deep, fast moving agricultural canals that crisscrossed the brown fields where I played with my sister and brother. On occasion we heard, with considerable panic, drama, and terror about the child, who while playing by the canal, slipped into the rushing water and flailed about trying to grab hold of the slick, slanted cement sides of the canal. The struggles were to no avail. Inevitably, the drowned child's body was found miles downstream. These dramatic events etched a deep, primal fear of the unknown into my subconscious mind—a fear that returned and escalated when I found myself slipping and sliding along an uncontrolled emotional canal rushing me downstream to a terrifying destination—over the edge into an unknown abyss.

Drinking my Way to the Bottom of the Heap

Soon after I landed my first big corporate job, I began to have some business success. It didn't come easily. With little formal education, I felt I needed to work extra hours to get onto an even playing field with my peers. I did like the challenge. I also loved the men, the parties, the cocktail hour, and the two-martini lunches. I was at the edge of the abyss and I didn't even know it yet. Success was like an exotic hallucinogenic drug, but it was never enough for me. It never lasted long enough.

A dark feeling of inadequacy haunted me. I worked and drank harder than anyone in the office. Soon I drank more than I worked. As I tumbled over the edge, I struggled to fight the downward spiral into my emotional abyss.

As long as I could get up in the morning, put on that conservative business suit, and get to the office with briefcase in hand, I was able to keep up a respectable and competent facade. I kept everyone believing that I was all right. Even as the powerful spiral sucked me more swiftly down toward ultimate destruction, I was able, day after day, to put on the corporate costume. I reassured everyone that I was doing just fine. After all, I was one of the young shining stars in the company.

Out of the office, my life was a shameful and devastating mess. After each episode, I would "get myself together," put on the corporate costume, put my business cards in my wallet (so I could remember who I was), and return to my desk.

I continued to show up with the corporate smile and continued to do the work better than many in my office. My co-workers continued to close their eyes to my dreadful emotional condition.

Daily living had become a torment. Against great odds, I had achieved the success I thought would bring happiness and peace of mind. Instead I felt suicidal and depressed. I had always considered insanity as a kind of perky zaniness that looked something like Goldie Hawn on *Laugh-In* or Jerry Lewis in one of his slapstick movies. When insanity struck me there was nothing light, funny, or zany about it. It was a bone-crushing, desperate, lonely despair. A heavy, black blanket covered my world. My very soul was being strangled. I was choking on a deep, dark mass rising up from the midst of my being. It was complete and utter hopelessness. Severe clinical depression seemed like a superficial medical description for how I felt. I had fallen into an abyss. There was no way out. The thought of living the rest of my life with this pain and soul sickness was unbearable.

I sought professional help. No one in my family had ever sought psychiatric help. I was the first and I was ashamed. I thought that this was evidence of some serious defect in me as a person. I blamed myself for not being strong enough to overcome my emotional shortcomings. I tried to keep my troubles from my co-workers, but I continued to spin downward and eventually, I attempted suicide. Of course, my employer and peers found out. But again, I was the 'master of deception.' I was able to return to work, briefcase in hand, with reassurances for everyone that it was over now, and I was fine. What was over? I didn't even know myself. My encounter with the abyss was certainly not over.

I was losing ground rapidly. I was now in a furious free fall into the unknown drowning darkness. I had no idea what was wrong and I was terrified. What could possibly be wrong now that I had a great corporate job? I was doing well. I had financial security and I had a company car, for God's sake? (I'd never even known anyone who had a company car.) I knew who I was—my business card told me that. I had the respect of co-workers. I had a nice place to live and I had more material things to give my kids than I'd ever had. Yet I was dying.

My fear of being labeled insane dominated all of my actions. Being insane would mean the end of my corporate life and the security I thought it promised me. I fought with all of my reserves, time and again, to put on the appearance of sanity and corporate respectability. Being sane was more important than anything in my life. If I couldn't keep the safety of the promised corporate security I wouldn't be able to care for my children. It was certainly more important than happiness or peace. *Work and worry*, my mother's mantra, had become my mantra. I didn't know I deserved happiness and peace. All my concerns were about appearances now and how the corporate world viewed and judged me.

With this powerful, destructive depression taking over all aspects of my life, I became totally self-centered. When concern about everything I did and said was the all-consuming problem, there was no time to think of anything or anyone else. This self-centeredness fueled the downward spiral and blocked out any possible rescue efforts. I turned inward. If a hand had been extended to pull me up, I could not have seen it.

I was sinking fast. There were many more suicide attempts, straight jackets, electro-shock treatments, and lock-ups. For brief periods of time, I would resume the corporate dance, but each time was shorter and more tenuous.

My co-workers were aware I had some problems, but I never let on about how bad things really were. By now I was the grand master of deception. I would show up with the corporate smile and tell them everything was fine. No one knew the depth of my despair. I'd be in the office on Thursday, for example, looking good, presumably doing well, meeting quota, ahead of the pack, and then, I'd go home and that very night, take an entire bottle of sleeping pills. No one understood. I didn't understand.

I fooled everyone: my peers, my family, even my psychiatrist. I showed up looking good one day in my psychiatrist's office and he decided that instead of therapy, I needed sex. This brought on a whole new set of disastrous emotional problems. I lost faith and trust in all human beings. I believed that everyone was interested in nothing but their own personal desires. I cut off all who might help me. I was alone.

The Bottom

When I finally hit bottom, I was still alive. That in itself was incredible. All my attempts to escape this human experience had failed. Only by staying alive until I hit bottom did I get the opportunity to learn a great lesson for living.

If you are free-falling into the abyss, the most important advice I can offer you is to stay with it and let go. Move into *Soul Survival* mode. You must let go of all of the old ideas that are strangling you. If you are facing corporate layoff or if you are miserably unhappy and unfulfilled in your corporate position, this can be your greatest moment. Corporate life is what we make it, but often our attitudes are full of fear. Fear blocks the light of reason and hope. Look around at the living examples. Everyone I know who has been downsized out or bludgeoned to insanity by corporate life and has had the courage to hang in there has, without exception, been brought to a new and more meaningful place in their lives.

Let go and wait. Your pain and fear will subside. You will wake up to a new and more rewarding life experience than you had ever thought possible. Remember, when one door closes, another opens. It's just the (sometimes long and dark) hallways between the doors that scare us to death. If a door has closed and you are in pain, be observant. Are your fingers in the closing door? Move them and let the door close. It's time to move on. The next adventure is beckoning.

Don't Let Fear Shut You Down

People said I was prone to 'acting out'. What a blessing. I couldn't have shut down if I had wanted to. I was the turtle without a shell. Frightened and depressed people who don't have the 'acting out' or suicidal nature often just shut down emotionally. They commit suicide quietly on the edge of the abyss, where they fearfully cling to their false ideas, their self-brewed realities, their imagined and rigid identities. They become the walking dead among us. We all know them. The corporate world abounds with them. They hang on and shut down. They may not have committed suicide by ending their physical lives, but they have strangled their souls and spirits. They have put in their time, gotten their paychecks, and if they're lucky, they stick it out until retirement.

These imprisoned spirits are disconcerting to anyone who knows them because they have lost their sense of openness, fun, and frivolity. The walls close in around these frightened souls, cutting off the light and joy of new fresh insights. Fear builds rigid barricades. Fear—fear of the abyss—causes them to cling to fanatical ideas. They cling to the edge, freezing into emotional and spiritual non-existence. They still breath, eat, and sleep, but for all intents and purposes their lives are over.

THE MASS OF MEN LIVE LIVES OF QUIET DESPERATION.
WHAT IS CALLED RESIGNATION IS CONFIRMED DESPERATION.
Henry D. Thoreau[1]

Getting Through the Abyss

When you're in an abyss, find a simple daily practice that will lighten your spirit and nourish your soul. A few years back when I was married, my husband fell into an abyss. At first he sank into a fearsome depression. His hopelessness colored every aspect of his daily existence. There seemed to be no way out. His business owed huge taxes and other seemingly insurmountable debts. In a state of desperation, he began praying every day. He had prayed throughout his life anyway, but this time he made a daily ritual of prayer, stopping every morning in a local church, getting down on his knees for a few minutes.

Within a week of beginning this new practice his attitude transformed. He saw his experience not as hopeless, but as a challenge. During the second week of his new practice, he came home and said, "I've worked too darned hard to

---

1.   Henry D. Thoreau, *Walden*, Houghton Miffin, 2004

just abandon this business. I'm going to make it work and I'm going to stick with it until it does." His entire outlook shifted from exhausted hopelessness to the energy of challenge. He felt positive and ready to deal with the problems his business faced, including the strong arm of the IRS and others who tried to intimidate him into submission.

We don't need to understand how spiritual principles work in order to practice them. Actually, most often, we don't understand how they work until we practice them. Simple, positive daily habits include things like reading something positive, praying, going for a quiet walk, or sitting peacefully for a short time with a positive thought. During this daily time of reflection, pay attention to everything. One at a time, look at every thought that comes to mind. Look and listen to your inner voice without an agenda, that is without some preconceived solution. All the answers we need lie within. We must provide a quiet time so we can hear our inner voice.

These little simple habits provide the lessons of the spirit life. When faced with abyss experiences, a number of my colleagues have done the same thing. I've been privileged to watch as simple daily practices transformed their lives.

By nurturing our souls daily, we are given new strength and insight to deal with seemingly hopeless situations. Don't give up. Instead, listen within for the amazingly simple spiritual answer.

A Belief System

Belief was a subject of much confusion for me for most of my early life. Only after my first abyss experience did I develop the beginnings of a real, personal belief system. It's nothing someone else could have given me. For me it was a personal *soul-lesson*.

A friend of mine is fond of reminding anyone questioning the existence of God that 90 percent of the people throughout the world believe in something. Do you want to be part of the miserable minority? I don't know if it's God, Buddha, Mohammed, The Great Spirit, Jesus, or the Virgin Mary, but I am sure, deep in my soul where all truth resides, that there is a divine power and it is good. I know this because I have been to the abyss. I am content with my limited concept of the divine because I know beyond any doubt it is real. I have been to the abyss and survived only because of the great and loving hand of this spiritual power.

I have also learned along the way that I am less afraid and happier when I define this divine power as personal. For me, this power is personally and intimately involved with my little insignificant issues. Other people are happier with a more intellectual power. In the abyss where I finally defined peace and happiness as my ultimate desire, I no longer relied on someone else's idea or definition of the divine power that brought them happiness. Once I rested quietly at the bottom, I was at last free to explore my own concept of a spiritual existence.

Surviving the corporation without a belief in something can be a very lonely business.

The Corporate Soul Survival Lesson

Let go and surrender your way to corporate success and peace of mind. The fall to the bottom will come more quickly if you can relax and let go. Try not to be afraid of the bottom. I know, *easier said than done*. It's very hard to not grasp desperately at the sides as you free fall through the abyss, just as the child struggled in the canal in my hometown. The lesson from the drowning child is clear. When you let go and relax, you will be able to see and take hold of the mysterious hands held out to you. The hands will soften your blow and rescue you from doom.

Although I'm not an expert on spirituality, I know there is an energy that we humans cannot see. It's an energy far more powerful than any energy created by mankind. This energy is a powerful and positive force when enough people strive toward it. It is an energy so bright and mighty that once enough people are on the path, it becomes a wave of positive power that brings about miracles.

When I hit bottom, I was broken and battered, but I had stopped fighting. The relief was monumental. The world suddenly and unexplainably became much more clear. I no longer needed to be sane; I just needed to be at peace. There at the bottom, I surrendered. If I was insane, so be it. I just wanted to be out of the battle. I abandoned all my phony ideas about corporate appearances and sanity. I became willing to move forward as an authentic, fragile, and vulnerable human being and businesswoman.

Everything I sought in the corporate world was available to me in my own soul. Peace and happiness did not reside in some other person, in a promotion, or in my corporate identity. The journey toward this happiness had to be my own personal pilgrimage.

Another Lesson from the Abyss

Humility is a character builder for corporate success, happiness, and inner peace. No, I'm not kidding. Humility is not about weakness. It is the core of spiritual strength.

As a woman driven by success, I didn't strive toward humility, but it turned out to be a peaceful oasis on my power-drive toward position and achievement.

Humility is not the same as humiliation. It is about being humble. Humility is an awareness of my own size (vulnerable and fragile) and my limited understanding of God, of other people, and the world around me. In seeing God and the world through the eyes of humility, I began to see how shortsighted I had been in my egotistical assumptions about God, humankind, and the experience of the *journey of life.*

For most of my corporate life I tried to figure out what to do next based on my internal spiritual and emotional guidance. I would not ask for help, fearing that I would be labeled as ignorant. I believed that my personal rationale, spiritual belief, and logic were common to everyone. Everything I did came out of this self-centered view of life. Since we're all created by the same divine source, I reasoned, surely at our depth, we must be all the same and desire the same peace of heart. If I knew the true way I was feeling about something, then you too must recognize that same spiritual truth.

This was an emotionally and spiritually self-centered approach to dealing with life. When someone finally pointed out to me that others didn't feel exactly like I did, I was blown away. The truth registered with an eye-opening thud. When I finally got it, I was amazed to see how much I had done in my life out of my own self-involved consciousness. At the same time, I felt a new freedom in replacing my self-limiting ideas with trust in a higher consciousness. Trusting in this powerful spiritual consciousness meant I didn't have to have all of the right answers.

I had thought humility was a sign of character weakness, but the opposite is true. With humility, we become stronger and more assertive. We are able to see the true importance of our everyday decisions and take new risks to assert our ideas. We are able to see the greatness of our existence.

Humility is one of the only traits that requires us to simultaneously acknowledge our greatness and our fragility. I realized that I was not nearly as big, powerful, and important as I thought. With humility, this is a good feeling. It's a relief. It removes the burden of needing to be right and needing to win. I'm just a small, fragile person in a big world. I can only do the best I can do at the time. I can take a risk based on whatever I know at the time. When I have humility, I realize that I may be making a mistake, but it won't be the end of the world. I can always change course further down the road when I have new information. This philosophy grants me the spiritual freedom to travel along my life path with confidence. I have everything I need for peace, happiness, and success.

Humility is a character asset to strive for. It turns out to be the peaceful reassurance of the truth of our purpose and existence. Humility is the gift of seeing myself, the world, and you, through the eyes of a spiritual reality.

Climbing Out of the Abyss

At the bottom of the abyss, I did the first honest inventory of my life. It was clear that any level of peace or achievement would be unattainable for me unless I could stop drinking and partying. There wasn't room in my life for motherhood, corporate achievement, and the fast-lane corporate party life. I was clearly addicted to alcohol and it was ruining my life. I was young and wanted to have a good time, but my good times had taken precedence over everything else and I was unable to control myself. I had to let go. I had to admit defeat. I had to ask for help. I had to restructure my life. In honestly evaluating myself, I opened the doorway to the first peace and happiness I had ever known. Self-honesty is the gateway to the spiritual life. It is also the key to all emotional growth.

Inventories are essential in every corporate life, crisis or no crisis. As we grow, we need to see where we are and where we are going by taking a good honest look at our strengths and weaknesses. This first inventory was straightforward.

My First Inventory

What I *was* Good At:	What I *wasn't* Good At:
Sales	Corporate politics
Dealing with quotas	Controlling managers
Relationships with customers	Expense reports
Building trust	Administrative duties
Following through	Following directions

In retrospect, I see that this first inventory was very basic and ignored most issues that could lead to happiness and peace, but it was the best I could do at the time. It served a good purpose. It gave me a sense of myself and my career strengths, as well as helping me to formulate a vision of where I could to go with training and perseverance.

The lessons of my first abyss experience were about honesty, peace, love, happiness, and letting go. These alone were—and remain—the goals. For me, surrender had been my saving grace. I have since heard it said that God is closest to us when we are at our lowest points. It was certainly true for me. Now for the first time I knew beyond doubt that there was a merciful and loving Creator. Only by that grace could I find peace in the midst of complete chaos.

After that first tumble into the abyss, I climbed higher than any woman had ever climbed in my company. I broke national sales records and became the first woman to achieve corporate recognition. I earned a membership in the prestigious Presidents' Club and won honors time and again for setting sales records.

The abyss fall is an all-consuming, self-centered time. This is neither bad nor good. It just is. The delicate center part of the soul needs attention. Give it what it needs and it will pass. When it does, the self-centeredness dissipates naturally, as a song of joy begins to form once again in the depth of your heart and soul.

8

The Abyss: A Dark Night
of the Soul

Mid Life Crisis—My Second Abyss

"Life is difficult," were the first words in *The Road Less Traveled*, the now famous book by Scott Peck[1]. I might add to those wise words, "Corporate life can be not only difficult, it can be emotionally crushing." Many people come to mid-life facing challenges they couldn't even have imagined. This mid-life crisis seems to affect most human beings. For those in the corporate arena, a mid-life crisis might come in the form of losing a job, a visit from the IRS, a business failure, being demoted, or facing lawsuits.

Maybe the mid-life crisis so many of us face really is the impetus for spurring us on to make greater spiritual contributions to the world. Without this *major kick in the ass*, we would most likely wander through our lives blindly and numbly, never noticing our souls, much less answering their beck and call.

As I approached age 48, I was confident in my dealings with myself and those around me. After 25 years on the corporate road, I felt that I had gained complete knowledge and control of myself and my abilities in business. I had reached an applaudable level of corporate success. I had the admiration of my peers and was respected in my industry. I falsely assumed that as a sophisticated, mature, and experienced businesswoman, I had the moxie and wisdom

---

1.   Scott Peck, *The Road Less Traveled* Touchstone Books, 1988

to handle any business situation that crossed my path. I couldn't have been more wrong.

In the early 1990s, I was engulfed in a major intellectual property owner-ship lawsuit. I had contributed to the design of a thriving software product and after years of work, two of the partners claimed ownership of the software source code and hence the product itself. Being involved in this leading edge legal battle was at the same time fascinating and emotionally devastating. I felt thoroughly betrayed by former partners. I felt they had stolen from me what was rightfully mine. I chastised myself for my weakness.

This was happening at the same time that I was struggling to 'get it right' for a manager who criticized me for being too enthusiastic, and for doing too much. I felt that with this manager, the work habits that had consistently brought me success were suddenly useless. I was at a loss for what to do to turn the situation around. This was the same person who practiced *management-by-criticism* and pitted his employees against one another to keep them weak and isolated. I felt my spirit being sucked out of me. My confidence was chal-lenged at every level.

When I went to my family doctor for a routine appointment in July 1993, my blood pressure was so high that the doctor put me on medical leave. He prescribed reading, gardening—anything to help me relax. How could this have happened to me? In twenty-five years, I hadn't ever been home without having some form of business work to do or think about. I went into shock. By week three on disability, I was in worse shape than when I had stopped work. What was wrong? Not working left me with hours on end to fret and worry about what would become of me. The fast-paced, numbing corporate life was all I had ever known. Without constant activity, challenges, drama, and excitement, I was faced with daily boredom and rising fear. My anxieties grew more pressing each day. What was intended as *relief* from corporate pressures left me facing an inner emotional turmoil I hadn't known existed. I only knew myself as a career-driven creature. I was the person on my business card.

I didn't realize it until years later, but the intense betrayal I experienced with my former business partners combined with my power-hungry boss play-ing games with my head, had triggered memories of deeply buried wounds that I had all but forgotten. It was a lethal combination.

Flashbacks

August 1993–It was a glorious Indian Summer day in California. The rolling hills surrounding the San Francisco peninsula were a delicate golden brown, signaling shorter, colder days to come. The air was light and warm. It was a day in life to be celebrated. I was on my way to the podiatrist and I had just turned onto Sand Hill Road, the avenue of Silicon Valley venture capitalists.

Suddenly my hands began to tremble. Sleep deprivation must have been taking its toll, I reassured myself. I had been on edge for so long. Yet the trembling was worsening. I was shaking from my core. What was wrong? There was a pounding beginning in the center of my belly. Nausea was rising up from my stomach. What was happening to me? I'd had panic attacks, but this was different. It was far worse. It was so out of control. Perspiration was poring off my forehead. I was reeling with dizziness and I needed to pull over. As my car edged toward the curb, the nausea worsened. Something was pounding deep inside of me. I could feel something physical, deep, and rhythmic. It was his penis. My psychiatrist! It had happened when I was 25 years old and I could feel him in me now. I opened the car door and heaved everything in my stomach. Vile, rotten waste spilled to the ground by the side of the road. Sobs rose out of my bruised and buried soul, sobs of an incident I had forced into the recesses of my mind for over 20 years. I knew I was having a breakdown, but I was a successful businesswoman. I couldn't do this now; I was a woman who was assertive and capable. I made decisions that started new companies and drove entire industries. I dealt with executives at every level of business. I transacted million-dollar deals. I was an independent and successful woman and I was crumbling under the weight of a mysterious force beyond my strength or understanding.

Getting Help

Six weeks after my corporate departure, I finally sought professional help. Completely unaware of deep-seated unresolved emotional problems, I went into a therapist's office and told my desperate tale. I had not slept more than two hours a night for nearly six months. I had chronic colitis. I was beginning to consider suicide and I could find no possible reason to be in such crippling pain. As it turned out, I was running from a past I couldn't bear to face and the corporation had been my hiding place.

The therapist was good. Fortunately he knew much of my history and he explained the sexual abuse issues that I had discounted, denied, and brushed off long ago. My first psychiatrist, a person I had trusted to protect me at all costs, had used me for his own personal desires. He had betrayed a pure and precious part of my soul. I had been too embarrassed and afraid to acknowledge the pain of the incident and I was unaware of the lasting lethal scars it had left.

I thought this experience was ancient history.

WHAT YOU PUT BEHIND YOU,
YOU PULL BEHIND YOU UNTIL YOU HEAL IT.

I thought I was far too sophisticated to get drawn into this messy emotional bog. I never really dealt with the betrayal, lack of trust, and shame these experiences had caused, and now, so many years later, I had been thrust into an abusive situation with an employer and a stressful lawsuit that echoed that original experience.

The inner unhealed wound was festering toward eruption. I completely fell apart. The emotional pain devastated me. If felt as if someone was ripping my heart out by the roots. It was unrelenting.

Friends and associates feared for my life. I did as well. I thought about suicide everyday. I prayed my car would careen headlong into a freeway barrier. I couldn't sleep. I was unable to communicate with anyone. I felt as if my physical body was flying apart. I was living a constant nightmare. I would drift off to sleep at night and awaken 30-45 minutes later, sweating, shaking, terrified, and unable to get back to sleep. When I finally did fall asleep, some protective barrier in my mind would fall and I would be flooded with agonizing fear. I began to lose my balance and fall down. Finally, I fell and fractured my leg. I was unable to go anywhere or do anything. Panic attacks became a regular event. With my heart pounding uncontrollably, I would gasp for breath and wonder if I was going to die. I burst into tears at the least provocation.

I began to have vivid flashbacks of incidents long ago buried. Out of nowhere, I would see horrifying, realistic scenes from a past I wanted to forget. Driving down the freeway, I'd suddenly have a flash back and have to pull over. It was as if all of my mind's defense systems had collapsed. I'd become hysterical with fear. I was sure I was going mad.

I was in this miserable state when a dear friend who had been to Vietnam talked with me one day. When I tried to relate what was happening, he said it sounded like *Post-Traumatic Stress Syndrome*. He gave me some literature about nurses who'd been in Vietnam and had never acknowledged the pain of what they had seen. It was comforting to see that others had had similar symptoms. I was not alone. A spark of hope ignited. There might be a way out of the pain.

Judy, the friend who had been my business partner, was in the lawsuit with me. (We were suing our former associates.) Although Judy and I had had our differences in the past, throughout this trying time, she became a sustaining resource for me. During this dark experience, she never let me forget the talents I had and what we had accomplished in business. She always had a reassuring word of confidence in my ability. At a time when I could barely think about living another day, these words of confidence were like a refreshing tonic.

For the next year I had to unravel excruciatingly bitter memories and expose them to the light of day for healing. I was unable to work, communicate, sleep, or eat almost anything. My fear and pain were all-encompassing. Each morning, I would awaken—no, I would get out of bed, since I hadn't slept all night—and sit on the side of the bed with tears of despair rolling down my cheeks. My husband stood by helplessly, trying to reassure me that I would feel good again someday.

Fighting Back for Healing

Right or wrong, in the midst of this crisis, I made the decision to confront and sue the psychiatrist who had abused me 20 years earlier. A series of coincidences—or miracles—had me talking with a lawyer who specialized in this type of professional abuse case. He said 20 years was far beyond the Statute of Limitations, but he thought there might be good defense for why it took so long for me to realize the impact of what had been done to me. The anger that

I had ignored and denied for so long, the anger that I had been so afraid to express, needed to be acknowledged. Only then could the soothing sweet freedom of forgiveness begin.

I don't know if this course of action would be right for any one else, but for me it proved to be a miracle of healing. During the next 12 months, I reviewed all of the evidence and horror of my experiences with this man. At a deposition, I had the opportunity to sit across the table from him and express my pain and the damage his actions had caused in my life. Only by bringing the worst horror and pain in my soul out into the light of day, were my wounds able to begin healing.

As the events around suing my psychiatrist unfolded, the gift I received was far greater than financial reward. I did win a small settlement, but it was nothing compared to the peace of mind I attained and now have. What a tremendous relief to be free of the ghosts that haunted my soul for so many years.

After this confrontation, I learned that most women who suffer this type of abuse situation end up committing suicide. I understand why. The pain was indescribable and I felt like there was no one I could turn to or trust. I was blessed in my healing and fortunate to be surrounded with many understanding and caring people.

All of us will get opportunities to heal our wounds, whether they are the wounds of yesterday or the submerged wounds of our childhood. To heal, we must remain open enough to explore them. The sunlight of truth can't open the blinds to our past unless we allow ourselves to be vulnerable. This can be a scary proposition, but honesty, truth, and awareness are the healing balm for all human problems. I know I can't hide out and pretend that everything is okay anymore. Whatever the consequences, we need to walk in the healing light of truth.

I feared that I would never return to the work world—the world that had been my motivation and my identity for most of my life. The corporate world had been a shield from the turmoil of my childhood. Corporate life had put a costume on me, a phony costume that told me and the world that by some crazy standard of appearances, I was doing okay. No wonder I loved the conservative suits and carrying the briefcase. It was both armor and mask, protecting me from the damaged part of my soul. Ironically, at the same time, it protected me from my pain; the camouflage effectively distanced me from my core-self.

The Corporate Soul Survival Lesson: Warts and All

In the emptiness at the bottom of the abyss, you will discover your basic personal and spiritual components. Only while lying flat on your back at the bottom, can you look up to see the light of a new day.

As I began the journey back from this dark and desperate place, I realized that I had spent a lifetime believing that 'getting well' meant being strong. I began to understand that 'getting well' means being vulnerable. I am just another small and fragile, garden variety, human being. This open admission of vulnerability seemed dangerous for someone trying to succeed in business. It ran contrary to everything I knew about corporate survival. But I was at a crisis point. I couldn't avoid this truth. If I wanted to experience a spiritually rich and real life, I could no longer put on the corporate costume and pretend to be who I was not. I could no longer—as I desperately wished I could—separate my personal self from my corporate self. I was *not* two different people. I needed to be one integrated spirit, warts and all.

Not everyone has such rock-bottom experiences, but most of us do face major hurdles at different points in our lives. These hurdles may relate directly to our corporate lives or they may be personal, but the influence still spills over into our business lives.

I was fortunate to have many people around me who loved and accepted me just the way I was. They didn't chastise me or minimize what I was going through. They just stood beside me and let me know they cared. Most supportive of all, they didn't pressure me to heal any faster than I could. I was blessed also with a wise and caring therapist who let me hurt for just as long as I needed to hurt. Throughout this entire ordeal I always knew that my therapist, my husband, and my friends would do anything they could to stop the pain, to save me. But they, too, were powerless.

Climbing Out of the Abyss Again

Success and overcoming trials often come by just following directions. These might be the directions of someone who has already had the experience or of someone who has had success in that area. Too frequently, our egos tell us we are unique, that we must find our own separate answers. We are *different*. In some circumstances this is true, but there is great wisdom in learning to follow the directions of others who have successfully overcome some great trial. When I gave up booze, I did it by following the directions of others who had overcome this devastating condition. I could not have done it by myself. Many other burdens in my life have been eased when I learned to ask for and receive help from others.

When Falling Into an Abyss, Seek Out Your Fans

Each of us has three categories of fellow soul travelers: fans, critics, and neutrals. If you have stepped off the cliff, if you are in a free fall to a dark and frightening abyss of your own, you need your fans around you. Your fans are those soul mates who love you unconditionally. They provide the soothing comfort that will heal your deep spirit wounds and allow you to open courageously to new possibilities that occur in *abyss experiences*.

While I was caught in the phase of continuous self-flagellation, in my *pull-yourself up by the bootstraps* mode, I often sought out my critics; thinking they would offer me ways to improve myself, do better, and thus end the fear, pain, and powerlessness of the abyss. When no help was forthcoming, I moved to neutral territory. I moved among the people who didn't care about me one way or the other and tried to act like everything was fine with me. This tactic was lonely, scary, and non-productive. It was the same old corporate camouflage I had used many times before. I no longer had the strength or desire to wear my phony corporate costume. In an emotional free-fall, critics and neutrals provide you nothing. They offer the false hope of power through achievement.

When I was flailing at the bottom of the last abyss, I sensed that I needed to seek out my fans. I identified my fans. Judy was one, my husband another. Barbara, Linda, Lori, and a select group of close friends, certain business associates, and even some corporate clients were fans. Even my therapist and my lawyer were fans, albeit paid fans. That was okay. Their unswerving devotion felt supportive. These people provided a soothing and protective cloak for my fragile self-esteem. I needed to see me through *their* eyes. I called old customers and corporate peers, some of whom I hadn't seen in years. I met with them. I told them the truth about my circumstances. I asked if they would write letters of recommendation for my portfolio. I had no idea what I would do with the letters or the portfolio, but they wrote the letters and I put them in the portfolio. Those letters and that portfolio became a foundation for healing my soul and my career. My contact with these fans started a process of restoring my battered self-esteem. The fans gave me new hope and insight about myself and my journey. The portfolio provided reassurance of the possibility of a new and brighter day if I could just hold on. Achievement power is an illusion in the abyss. The only power to keep you from drowning in the desperate despair of this dark night of the soul is love and surrender.

More Lessons

As I recovered from that dark night of the soul, I learned powerful spiritual lessons. I became aware that no matter how much other people cared for me, they could not possibly understand or feel the pain in my heart. Maybe we never really understand another person's pain. I don't think our purpose is to understand. The overall purpose for our souls is to learn to love one another unconditionally. So we can give up trying to be all-understanding, sympathetic people. We can just accept and love. Love is the healing energy. Understanding another soul's pain and darkness is difficult at best. I'm only capable of feeling my own feelings. I may have had similar feelings to yours, but I can never be sure that you feel those feelings exactly the way I do. It doesn't matter. It's not important. My purpose is to love and accept.

The other significant lesson of this dark experience was the value of hope. Unlike my first trip into the abyss, this time I had intellectual knowledge of it, born of experience. I had been there before and I had survived to live stronger and happier than before. I had experienced a new dimension of spiritual peace. I had hung on long enough for the pain to pass. In my first trip to the abyss, I had tried to kill myself several times. I didn't know there would ever again be light, joy, and laughter. The second time, although it felt dark and hopeless, I knew that I might laugh and sing again if I could just hang on long enough.

A wonderful prayer I heard that says it all:

DEAR GOD,
THANK YOU FOR LETTING ME LAUGH AGAIN,

BUT PLEASE DON'T EVER LET ME FORGET THAT I CRIED.

A Personal and Professional Inventory

In 1993, I surrendered to the second abyss. At the bottom, I could look at my true strengths, my desires, and my weaknesses with amazing clarity. I did a second inventory. This time it addressed both personal and professional issues. I acknowledged the importance of my corporate attributes, and I assessed what I really wanted to do with the rest of my life. There were things I did fairly well but didn't enjoy doing. I was nearly 50 years old. The course ahead was shorter. It was time to outline for myself what I enjoyed doing and what I could contribute in the time I had left.

My Inventory looked like this now:

I do these things well	I don't do these things well	I like to do these things	I don't like to do these things	I am comfortable doing these
Sales	Politics	Mentoring	Quotas	Training
Quotas	Controlling	Speaking	Details	Speaking
Relationships	Management	Training	Following instructions	Writing
	Administrative			

In this second professional inventory, I acknowledged that I had twenty-five years of experience in my field. These twenty-five years represented a wealth of experience, knowledge, and education that younger people needed. Many were hungry for the guidance I could give them.

A Word to Those Facing Mid-Life

If you are at a mid-life turning point as I was, examine the years of experience you already have. They are your assets. If you have been doing something for a few years, as most of us have by mid-life, then we probably know a lot more than we think we do. We possess valuable knowledge and experience that is sorely needed by younger people entering our business. Young people bring exciting new technology, ideas, and intelligence, but they desperately need the wisdom and experience of those who have gone before them. If you are facing mid-life, you have this wisdom.

Whether you are a worker on the manufacturing line, an administrative assistant, a sales manager, a corporate trainer, an executive, a marketing specialist, a salesperson, or any other businessperson, you know more than you think you know. After all, you have survived this long. You've learned many of the tools. You have perseverance and know its value. You have mental toughness that comes from consistently showing up. This is the bedrock of your future.

Most of us take the daily tasks we have been performing for so long for granted. We need to stand back and take an objective look at how experienced we are and how well we know the ropes of our corporate position. Somewhere right under your nose is a young person, just starting out in corporate life. He/she needs your strength, wisdom, and guidance.

At mid-life, I realized that if I was to accomplish my dreams, I needed to get started. The incentive isn't fear, but a positive awareness that my best and most fruitful years are ahead of me. I must make a beginning and surely, now is the time to go for it.

In the chaos of today's cutthroat corporate layoffs and downsizing, many people are building whole new careers out of their knowledge and experience base. They're crafting careers for themselves that are infinitely more rewarding than anything they've ever done before.

So examine your strengths, your spiritual gifts, the things you do well. Dream about using those strengths to build a new (spiritual) corporate life for yourself. There are many young people who need your love and experience. Repackage yourself and build yourself a new life and career or reinvent your current career to create the life you desire.

If you did the suggested inventory of your strengths and weaknesses, look in the columns where you wrote the *things you like to do* and the *things you are comfortable doing*. This is where you should direct your attention. In the long run, this is where you will be most successful, both financially and personally.

I decided to start my own business doing what I did best, which was training and motivating business people. I had been writing a magazine column about this topic for some time, so I already had laid a few bricks on the path. I thought I might enjoy this work. I called on some faithful business associates and set up a pilot class to see how it would work and how I could contribute to the careers of others. It went well. I was encouraged, and I moved ahead from there.

More Value From the Abyss: There Are No Mistakes in Life, Only Lessons

The finest and most cherished parts of my professional and private self were honed out of me in my abyss experiences. They were the essence of character building. Stay vulnerable and you won't find yourself hanging over the ledge of an abyss, frozen solid in your fear. Try not to be afraid. The ride is just an adventure of discovery. It is a discovery of your soul-self, the eternal you.

You may not feel it is safe or smart to be completely open and vulnerable to those around you, but do stay vulnerable to the lessons of life that come your way every day. You are on the right path. Remember that, even when everything seems to say you have strayed far off course. There are no mistakes in the life we are given, only lessons. These lessons are meant to grow our souls. Character building isn't easy but it's always rewarding. Don't let fear shut down your spirit for adventure.

On my life path, my lessons from the abyss are the ones of the greatest importance, not only to me, but also to those around me who are sharing my present experience. Your lessons and my lessons are the wisdom and truth of the ages demonstrated though our life experiences. They are the very essence of what is real in my life and yours. These lessons are the incredible thread that ties my soul to yours. These honest true-life experiences connect human beings at the heart level.

I don't understand your pain or joy. I don't even know myself as well as I could. Eight or nine years of therapy have opened some inner chambers, but surely much of the love and greatness in my soul is yet to be revealed. I know that no human being can actually feel the pain of another nor completely understand the causes of that pain. Our real task as humans is not to understand but to love. We needn't fret about developing more compassion. Remember, we are just little people on a great adventure. We will develop the qualities we need for our unique journeys through all the experiences in our corporate and personal lives.

Who You Are is Who You Are

The corporate world is a dysfunctional environment where fierce competition, fear, and a certain brutality can be the norm. The corporate world defines you by the motto, "What you do is who you are." This is a bald-faced lie. *Who you are is who you are.* You are the great spirit that exists within you, the spirit that is bursting to get on with this adventure called life. Dance to *your* drummer, not mine or anyone else's. Your drummer knows your tune.

I believe there is basic goodness in all human beings. Beneath whatever corporate costume we may wear, lies the goodness of mankind. When brutal competition and the pursuit of pure financial profit drive the corporate world, the very soul of all mankind suffers from loneliness and isolation. This separation of people's spirits causes intense sorrow and failure. This failure of the corporation is also a failure of the individual and failure of mankind itself.

The only power you and I have involves failure of the individual. We have the power to realize that we have a choice. We can choose to listen to our spirit and respond. We can believe in who we are and see our greatness. Only the spirits of individuals can propel the corporate world to soaring and meaningful success.

A Final Story from the Abyss: Miracles Happen in the Abyss

Spring 1995—Miracles happen in the abyss. Things happen there that could only happen when we're in that uniquely open, vulnerable, trusting, and attentive state of mind. Here's a story about someone else coming back from the abyss. It started out with my regular routine.

Sunday morning, the sun was bright and spring was bursting on my little quiet street. Gardens were springing forth with blossoms of all colors and fragrances. With Walkman and running shoes, I took off for my morning jog. My spirit was soaring and my heart was singing. What a day! I was so glad to be alive.

At the downtown coffee shop, I met a good friend enjoying the morning sunshine and the strong espresso coffee. This man was once a corporate leader. He rode the corporate highway to success, but a few years ago he fell into the abyss. On this day he sat serenely sipping coffee. In front of him was a beautiful wood box, obviously a hand-crafted work of art.

"What is this," I asked.

He chuckled and said, "Let me tell you a story. As you know, I've been at the bottom of this abyss for some time. It's been a weird but not unpleasant experience. Ever since I fell into this abyss on my corporate journey, I've been trying to figure out what to do with my life."

"About a year ago, my old clunker automobile needed some smog work. I took it in for repair. After days and days, the mechanic finally called me in and said it would cost way too much to repair, but maybe I would want to do the work myself. Since I'm at the bottom of this abyss, I've got time on my hands and figure I might as well. They gave me all of the instructions, step by step."

"I took the old wreck home. I spent weeks getting everything done according to the instructions. Finally, putting all the pieces back together, I tried it out. *Oh my God, it was worse!*"

"All that work and I'd left out one of the most important parts, some deeply buried engine gasket. I couldn't face trying to do it all over again. I surrendered and decided, for the time, I would just ride my bike."

"About this time, I got a job offer from an old associate in a high-tech Silicon Valley firm. I weighed the pros and cons. Reasons I should take the job: money, greed, prestige, ego. The list of reasons I shouldn't take the job was about three pages long. I declined the job, which I figured was either an act of pure stupidity or some kind of moral courage."

"Life does go on and one day while leisurely riding my bike around the bottom of the abyss, I noticed something I never would have seen from my speeding car: A local resident, who imported rare and unusual woods. He imported these woods from all over the world and sold them to US companies for building fine musical instruments. We started chatting and when I told him I had once done some work with fine woods, he gave me some scraps."

"Within days, an acquaintance approached me and asked if I had room to store some tools of his. He said I could use them if I wanted to. He wasn't sure he'd ever need them again. The tools included several fine saws, worth thousands of dollars, for doing exotic and precision design work with wood. I went home and began to design a handcrafted wooden box."

As he sat in front of the coffee shop that morning, my friend beamed with pride as I admired his latest box. It was a piece that would sell for several hundred dollars. His craftsmanship was certainly enough to provide the beginnings of a new creative and prospering livelihood for this man and his family. More important was the pride and pleasure he got from this creative expression of his unique and talented spirit. Coincidence? I don't know. The bottom of the abyss is filled with stories like his.

Courage is gained through showing up when the path ahead is not cleared. The road is less traveled. This is the adventure. Through this letting go, hanging in there, and putting one foot in front of another, a door ahead opens—invariably a door to a new and unexpectedly rewarding experience of the spirit.

9

Principle Five—Trust: Living in the Light of Divine Destiny

Defining Moments in Soul Success

May 2000, Chicago—I was invited to speak at the Enlightenment 2000 conference in Chicago. Enlightenment 2000 is a media seminar sponsored by well-known Chicago company, Activia. The company, a leader in providing technical professionals to large corporations, was founded about five years ago by a young woman entrepreneur named Susan Perlitz.[1] She had built a business with notable clients like Lucent Technologies, United Airlines, Motorola, Nicor Gas, and University of Chicago. Susan founded Enlightenment 2000 to bring together professionals in the technology industry for networking, new product knowledge, and motivation. For Susan, the conference was one of those amazing inspirational ideas with which entrepreneurial spirits are both burdened and blessed.

Together with her staff, Susan worked on preparations for the conference for months. They got good press on the conference. They sought out speakers of national and local acclaim. They made deals and set up a great program. They hired experts to make all the on-site logistical arrangements. They worked night and day, using all their energy and resources. However, the Enlightenment 2000 conference had never been done before. Actually, a con-

---

1. This name, as well as the name of the company and the conference have been changed

ference of this nature had never even been attempted, but with her courageous and optimistic spirit, Susan saw past all the obstacles. She focused on her dream, her higher vision: the coming together of this inspiring group of professionals.

I was lucky enough to be included in the program with my friend, Basha, who comes from Columbia Broadcasting School in Chicago. Our presentation was titled "Self-Marketing with a Passion."

On conference day, Susan sent a driver for the presenters. She had us there by 7:00 A.M. so we would have time to make final preparations with equipment, programs, rooms, and all of the last-minute details that enable seminars to run smoothly. A nationally acclaimed speaker from UPI (United Press International) in Washington, DC was there and a famous local singer came to present some inspiring entertainment. Everything was perfectly prepared.

As the opening hour of 9:00 A.M. approached, no attendees had arrived. Some of us questioned Susan about participant response. How many people would be there? She had her dream. She expected the rooms to fill easily with between 200 and 300 people. She had never done a conference before. At 9:10 A.M. some of us were still in that last minute, frantic quest to iron out all of the coordination and technical issues, when one of us all of a sudden realized that no one was there. Finally, the words were spoken aloud, "No one is here!"

After months and months of preparation, publicity, and work, not a single participant showed up. We began to realize the devastation that was unfolding. There was no one there. Susan's dream, months of work, enthusiasm, and planning were suddenly turning into a public nightmare of failure. What to do?

This is one of those defining moments that will surely happen to every entrepreneur. Your defining moment will not be the same experience as Susan's, but if you are an entrepreneurial spirit, that risk-taking, passionate, go-after-your-dreams kind of soul, then you will certainly have mountain top victories as well as those tragic moments. You will come to recognize how you handle these experiences will define your character, your success, and your future. Your attitude at these moments of tragedy, your response to these types of happenings, will set the course for future failure or success.

I have no doubt about Susan's future success. Her response to one of the most devastating experiences in her career (or maybe her whole life), was the attitude of a great and courageous spirit. She revealed the soul of a true leader. Her reactions and actions in the face of seemingly complete failure were a lesson for all of us that were privileged to be there on that fateful day.

As we crept out of our respective meeting rooms to try to bring words of comfort or wisdom to Susan, some of us were able to recall similar devastating experiences of our own, particularly those of us with the entrepreneurial bent. I had started a seminar business some years ago and initially had experienced the same puzzling lack of initiative with those I thought would flock to my seminar series. I learned how difficult this type of business can be.

We found Susan in the lobby, hunched over the registration table. Sobs wrenched her thin, ambitious shoulders. Cry, we told her. Let it out. She did—for a few minutes. Then, calling from within herself the character and determination of a true leader, she began to make lemonade out of lemons.

She spoke of all of the great publicity she had received as a result of planning the conference, including an outstanding write-up in an industry magazine that could be used for future campaigns. She realized that she had a cameraman all ready to go and a group of very impressive speakers. She asked everyone if they would allow her to interview each of them on film for future publicity. She got everyone in front of that camera and asked the questions that would produce headline video clips.

Although she could hardly smile about the experience, she took a devastating set of personal feelings and put them aside. She demonstrated the courage of a great businessperson. "If you have a dream," said Susan, "follow it and don't give up until you reach your goal." I have no doubt that Susan, Activia, and any other venture she conceives will fulfill her dreams and the dreams of many others.

IF YOU HAVE A DREAM, FOLLOW IT,
AND DON'T GIVE UP UNTIL YOU REACH YOUR GOAL.

She demonstrated beautifully the spiritual principles outlined in this book. I saw in Susan's experience the wisdom and truth of these simple principles. She had **persevered** to put this all together and now, faced with failure, she had no choice but to **be honest** about it. She was honest and vulnerable to all of us there. She had nowhere to hide. And as we watched, she **courageously owned her power** to choose a positive attitude and began to **gratefully see her blessings**. Then she looked after her employees and assured them this was just the beginning and only a faltering blip on the path of **divine destiny**.

In my own life and experiences as a businesswoman, I have learned that these moments of seeming failure are the moments that truly create your future. These are the experiences that take your soul to the heights of success and build a character of substance. These are the defining moments that come into every business life. These are the moments when greatness is born.

Spiritual Flow: The Five Soul Survival Principles

The five *Soul Survival* principles work together much like body, mind, and spirit flow together. I have separated each of the principles only for the purposes of discussion, but they are *all* required for living a spiritually meaningful life.

The Five Soul Survival Principles

1. Honesty: Opening the Door to Your Soul

2. Gratitude: Count Your Blessings

3. Courage: Owning Your Power to Choose

4. Perseverance: Hanging On in the Dark Times

5. Trust: Living in the Light of Divine Destiny

When you practice these five *Soul Survival* principles you'll discover one does not exist without the other. For example, if you don't practice the principle of staying honest, open, and vulnerable, you won't learn the lessons life brings because you'll be too busy telling little white lies about who you want others to think you are and creating barriers around your heart to keep yourself 'safe'. When you isolate yourself emotionally with a phony facade, you resign yourself to a shallow life, without the love, passion, and depth you experience when you are living a life in which you are genuinely yourself. If you don't practice daily gratitude, you will live in other negative feelings such as anger and fear. You will find it difficult to persevere or trust in anything. Each of the five *Soul Survival* principles interweaves with the others to bring about the life you have been dreaming of living.

Honesty

When you are honest with yourself at a very deep level, you clear the path for seeing greater truth. You strip away denial about the unhealthy beliefs that prevent you from taking responsibility for your behavior. Once you've uncovered the lies you've been telling yourself, you open yourself to seeing the truth.

Honesty heals. Honesty with myself around my family issues and the sexual abuse incident marked my emergence from shame. Once the shame subsided, I was free to heal and move on with my life. Truly, the things you hide from yourself and others keeps you in so much inner turmoil that you cannot connect with your divine destiny.

Gratitude

Recognizing the events—even the painful ones—that offer valuable learning experiences is essential to recognizing the markers along our spiritual path. Taken together and viewed with honesty, you will be able to see patterns in the jobs you accept, the people you encounter, and the struggles you have time and time again. When you look into these events for the lessons they offer you, the strengths they've built in you, you will see a larger pattern, a path that your life is taking. Accepting both joyful and painful events as valuable lessons broadens your sense of meaning and purpose.

Courage

When you recognize and embrace your own power, you stop allowing others to define you. You learn to differentiate between who you are and what happens to you. When you are in your own power, you can decide how to respond to situations that are beyond your personal realm of control. You begin to realize that your boss and the company you work for are not your source of power. Your power comes from within, and from trusting in the wisdom of divine destiny.

Power is the fuel that drives us along our path. Women need to learn not to fear power. We need to accept, deep in our hearts, that we have a right to our power. It may well be that as more women come to terms with their power, the rest of us will feel more comfortable stepping into ours.

Spiritual power is the belief and trust in your own inner greatness, as well as an alignment with a spiritual source outside yourself. *You are great.* Each person on earth is living out a preordained destiny with his or her own greatness. So many people get scared and shut down. They believe the disempowering lies the corporate world tells. These lies say you're limited or inferior. No one is inferior. Each human being is equipped with a set of powerful spiritual tools. The only limits are your beliefs.

Your spiritual journey should acquaint you with your inner gifts, those talents that are uniquely yours. The people you meet, the lives you touch, hold special meaning for you. No other soul is linked to the same people, the same set of encounters as you are. The people you work with are with you for a reason. Some of them will undoubtedly play significant roles in your development as a spiritual being.

Allow your personal greatness to shine out onto the world. You won't know how precious and powerful your personal talents are until you have risked exposing them to the world. You will do the world a great service by adding your authentic talents, rather than the hollow, passionless skills you may well be practicing now. As your authentic life-lights shine, it will feel that much safer for more timid souls to reveal their true talents.

I've said this before, but it bears repeating: your boss is not your power. The CEO is not your power. Don't give yourself over to those who would claim your power for material gain alone. Wherever you are in the corporate structure, you are still the power in your own life. You choose how you think and act. Maintain a sense of dignity and esteem in whom you are and what you have to contribute to the people around you. Corporations give more power to some people than others, but in the world of the soul, this is all nonsense. We are all just human beings, all capable of either trudging or dancing along the corporate road.

Perseverance

Life is about the journey not the destination. Perseverance is a kind of 'faith by doing'. You start by being there for yourself, day in and day out, trusting in positive outcome in the long term. Perseverance gets you out into the world, seeking opportunities and solutions to the challenges you've set for yourself. When you're among other people, you avail yourself of the miracles that happen when you're on your divine path.

It is valuable to set goals for yourself and to be willing to move toward them, but you shouldn't fixate on goals that are too rigid. If you are overly concerned when you miss such goals, you might condemn yourself as a failure rather than considering what you've learned along the way. Out of frustration, I gave up goal-setting altogether for a while when I was younger. Goals so often seemed just out of reach. Now I realize that achieving goals isn't nearly as important as who I became as I moved toward them. I'm no longer disappointed when specific goals don't materialize. I know that persevering and trusting divine destiny will get me where I'm supposed to go.

Trust in Divine Destiny

Does divine destiny, by definition, carry with it pre-ordained outcome? To some degree, yes. However, we can choose to stumble blindly along our paths, suffering life's seemingly meaningless cruelties or we can open our eyes and hearts, choosing to see more clearly. Using this sharpened vision, we develop the spiritual tools that help us to see further down our divine paths. We can begin to avoid some of the 'wrong turns' along the way and move more consciously and confidently toward fulfilling God's individualized plan for us.

The life I have yearned for, a life in which every minute counts, in which I see that everything I do is part of a larger spiritual journey and everyone I meet brings a lesson for my soul, is mine at last. I found this life within the corporate structure. The challenges and soul lessons I've learned in business helped me to evolve and eventually to flourish. I see my life not as a series of isolated events, but as an interconnected flow of spiritual experiences. I view business experiences as spiritual experiences, no less precious to me than my experiences with loved ones. Coming from this perspective, I am able to treat myself, my co-workers, and my workplace with the compassion, respect, dignity, and depth they deserve. My co-workers are fellow travelers on my spiritual path. *They are my students. They are my teachers.*

The Wave of Future Business is Forming Now: The Dream Society

The Information Age, which began only a few decades ago, is nearing its end, according to Rolf Jensen, Director of the Copenhagen Institute for Future Studies[2], and author of *The Dream Society*[3]. He predicts that in the years

---

2.   Copenhagen Institute for the Future, www.cifs.dk

ahead, we will move into what might be called the *Dream Society*, a society focused on dreams, spirituality, and feelings.

The highest-paid person in the first half of the next century, says Jensen, will be the storyteller. This theory seems quite plausible considering the tremendous popular appeal of books like *Chicken Soup for the Soul*[4] or IBM's recent commercials not about computers, but about people all over the world. Many other global companies are already storytellers in their marketing approach. Corporations will seek to capitalize on humanity's need to connect with one another, to overcome the coldness of isolation and loneliness of spirit.

Corporate strategy sessions increasingly focus on storytelling. In the future, according to Jensen, the general population's focus will shift from material to spiritual needs, from technology and science to emotions and storytelling. Strategic dreamers will help corporations understand the spiritual goals of potential customers, employees, and stockholders.

Today's companies are rational, efficient, and devoted to making profits because they developed out of the Industrial Age and the Information Age. According to Jensen, in the future, companies obsessed with efficiency and working only for profit will be regarded as untrustworthy. In the *Dream Society*, we will want to achieve certain human values. For example, kindness to animals, fairness to all, or happiness for workers and their communities. When our grandchildren look back on the lives we lived in the Information Age, they will see it as dull and gray, dominated by technology and the neglect of precious human values. They will understand that we couldn't free ourselves from our focus on work—work that we narrowly viewed as a means to pay for consumable goods and leisure pursuits.

---

3.   Rolf Jensen, *The Dream Society, How the Coming Shift from Information to Imagination will Transform Your Business*, McGraw Hill, 1999
4.   Jack Canfield, Mark Victor Hansen, *Chicken Soup for the Soul* series, Health Communications

"IN THE FUTURE, COMPANIES OBSESSED WITH EFFIENCY AND WORKING
ONLY FOR PROFIT WILL BE REGARDED AS UNTRUSTWORTHY."

There are already examples of corporations that practice care of human soul and spirit by placing decent and loving principles above all else. (Not that any corporation does this perfectly, but there is an essence of human importance driving many consistently successful corporations.) The underpinnings of these successful corporations will be driving principles delivering hope, dignity, and purpose to the individual employees who are walking the corporate path in the future. This sense of dignity comes about when each person is a contributor to the corporate purpose and hope is a byproduct of this dignity.

The 100th Monkey

Let me tell you about the legend of The Hundredth Monkey (Reprinted from a book by the same name written by Ken Keyes, Jr.[5]). Here is the story:

The Japanese monkey *Macaca Fuscata,* has been observed in the wild for a period of over 30 years. In 1952 on the island of Koshima, scientists were providing monkeys with sweet potatoes dropped in the sand. The monkeys liked the taste of the raw sweet potatoes, but they found the dirt unpleasant.

An 18-month-old female named *Imo* found she could solve the problem by washing the potatoes in a nearby stream. She taught this trick to her mother. Her playmates also learned this new way and they taught their mothers too.

This cultural innovation was gradually picked up by various monkeys before the eyes of the scientists. Between 1952 and 1958, all the young monkeys learned to wash the sandy sweet potatoes to make them more palatable.

---

5.   Ken Keyes, Jr., *The Hundredth Monkey,* Vision Books, 1989

Only the adults who imitated their children learned this social improvement. Other adults kept eating the dirty sweet potatoes.

Then something startling took place. In the autumn of 1958, a certain number of Koshima monkeys were washing sweet potatoes—the exact number is not known. Let us suppose that when the sun rose one morning there were 99 monkeys on Koshima Island who had learned to wash their sweet potatoes. Let's further suppose that later that morning, the hundredth monkey learned to wash potatoes. Then it happened!

By that evening almost everyone in the monkey tribe was washing sweet potatoes before eating them. The added energy of this hundredth monkey somehow created an ideological breakthrough!

But notice. A most surprising thing observed by these scientists was that the habit of washing sweet potatoes then jumped over the sea—colonies of monkeys on other islands and the mainland troop of monkeys at Takasak-iyama began washing their sweet potatoes!

Thus, when a certain critical number achieves a new awareness, this new awareness may be communicated from mind to mind. Although the exact number may vary, the *Hundredth Monkey Phenomenon* means that when only a limited number of people know of a new way, it may remain the consciousness property of these people. But there is a point at which if only one more person tunes-in to a new awareness, a spiritual energy field is strengthened, so that this awareness is picked up by almost everyone!

This phenomenon happened on an international level when in a single 12-month period in 1989, the world watched Communism being abandoned in the Soviet Union, the Berlin Wall coming down, apartheid ending in South Africa, and most of the Eastern Bloc countries freeing themselves from Communist rule. A wave of energy seemed to flow from continent to continent. Freedom was being sought on a larger scale than ever before in modern history.

Become That 100th 'Monkey'

You are far more important than you ever imagined. You are a part of this powerful energy field. As you continue to live by your values, your dreams, your love, your beliefs, and your ideals, your energy becomes part of a greater movement toward living genuinely. You carry in your hands and heart, the fuel for a profoundly improved new world.

As a single 'monkey' in the corporate world, it *appears as though* you have no power, but you have all the power, all the control. At some point, one of us will cross over and become the *Hundredth Monkey* in the practice of being our authentic selves and teaching others to be their authentic selves in their business lives. Imagine, if you can, the positive ramifications of honest communication, healthy relationships, and soul-sensitive products and services.

When enough souls in the corporate world have risen to a higher level, human consciousness will shift into a new phase, a phase where love, concern for human well-being, dignity, and equality will drive the profit stream of the business world.

Corporate success will result from the goodness, hope, dreams, and sense of purpose in each individual worker. Let the shift begin with you.

About the Author

Lynne Leahy has been honored as Entrepreneur of the Year in 2000 and 2001 by Working Woman Magazine. Her company, AquaPrix, Inc. has been recognized as one of the 100 Largest Woman Owned Businesses in the San Francisco Bay Area for several years. She has also been featured in many business publications including California CEO, Business Week, San Francisco Business Times, Silicon Valley Biz Ink, East Bay Business Times, and San Jose Business Journal.

Lynne has founded four previous companies in the document imaging and technology training industry. In that industry she was an international keynote speaker and, wrote and published three books, one of which was adopted as the industry standard. She has consulted and contracted with major corporations including Canon, Minolta, the CIA, Eastman Kodak, IBM, Xerox, Sharp Electronics, Amtrak, and many others.

As a corporate executive, Lynne was the first woman to be recognized by a Fortune 500 company as National Salesperson of the Year and the first woman in that company's prestigious President's Club in 1981.

She is also a tireless community volunteer. She serves on the Board of the Service League of San Mateo County, is a former Board Member of Women's Initiative for Self Employment (WISE) in San Francisco.

Lynne lives in San Carlos, California and is the President/CEO and Founder of AquaPrix, Inc. a health technology company in Hayward, California. She is 60 years old, has five children, eight grandchildren, and four great-grandchildren.

You can reach her at lynne@soul-survival.com

www.ingramcontent.com/pod-product-compliance
Lightning Source LLC
Chambersburg PA
CBHW030807180526
45163CB00003B/1171